ASCEND

ISBN 978-1-952320-02-6 (Paperback)
Ascend
Copyright © 2020 by Andy Jobe

Yorkshire Publishing
4613 E. 91st St,
Tulsa, OK 74137
www.YorkshirePublishing.com
918.394.2665

Printed in the USA

ASCEND

Climbing the Mountain of Discipleship Together

Who shall ascend the hill of the Lord?
And who shall stand in his holy place?
He who has clean hands and a pure heart...
Such is the generation of those who seek him, who
seek the face of the God of Jacob. *Selah*
Psalm 24:3–6

ANDY JOBE

TULSA

Acknowledgements

This workbook is not so much about the words that are written down as it is about the life behind the words - being discipled and discipling others. To that end I want to thank the people who have been with me all along the way: behind the scenes, encouraging me, praying for me, and discipling me.

My most special thanks goes to my family. My wife, Dustie, and my sons, Nolan, Mason, and O.B. have witnessed the disciple-making process fleshed out in my life and ministry. They know the real me and they have been sworn to secrecy.

I want to thank the countless people who walked with me on my pilgrimage throughout my ministry. The list is too long to print, but God knows your faithfulness. Pastors and professors, farmers and coaches, friends and family, I truly thank God for each of you.

I would like to thank all the churches who have allowed me to serve with them over the years. Each of you hold a special place in my heart. Thank you for allowing me to learn and grow along the way.

Finally, I want to thank Jesus. Thank you for saving me by Your grace and allowing me to serve You. I do not deserve either.

For Mom and Nanny.

2 Timothy 1:5

I am reminded of your sincere faith, a faith that
dwelt first in your grandmother Lois and your mother
Eunice and now, I am sure, dwells in you as well.

Table of Contents

Introduction

Go therefore and make disciples of all nations,
baptizing them in the name of the Father
and of the Son and of the Holy Spirit,
teaching them to observe all that I have
commanded you. And behold, I am with
you always, to the end of the age.
Matthew 28:19–20

Many of life's activities have a technical side and a **"just get to it"** side. Take fishing for instance. There are technical and scientific approaches to fishing: which lure to use, what rigging is best, fish finders, meteorology, and measuring water temperature. And then there is my son's approach: put a worm on the hook and throw it in the water. I have been fishing hundreds of times employing both methods and guess what? I have caught more fish by **"just getting to it"** than I have by monitoring water temperature and choosing the right lure.

Discipleship also has a technical aspect and a **"just get to it"** approach. It is easy to become bogged down in the cumbersome and tedious methodology of discipleship, when we really just need to **"get to it**." In fact, a legalistic approach to discipleship is possibly more harmful than not being discipled at all.

In the Judaism of Jesus' day it looked like this:

> But woe to you Pharisees! For you tithe mint
> and rue and every herb, and neglect justice
> and the love of God. These you ought to have
> done, without neglecting the others. Woe to
> you Pharisees! For you love the best seat in the
> synagogues and greetings in the marketplaces.
> Woe to you! For you are like unmarked graves,
> and people walk over them without knowing it.

One of the lawyers answered him, 'Teacher, in saying these things you insult us also.' And he said, 'Woe to you lawyers also! For you load people with burdens hard to bear, and you yourselves do not touch the burdens with one of your fingers.'   **Luke 11:42–46**

This kind of burdensome, legalistic religion prompted Jesus, in **Matthew 11:28-30**, to say, "Come to me, all who labor and are heavy laden, and I will give you rest. Take my yoke upon you, and learn from me, for I am gentle and lowly in heart, and you will find rest for your souls. For my yoke is easy, and my burden is light."

Over the years there have been many people who helped shape my spiritual identity. There was Cliff Fite, the Director of Missions at Kay Baptist Association in the 1980's. Cliff took me to church camp every year from the time I was eight years old until I graduated from high school. He was there when I was saved, baptized, called to ministry, married my wife, licensed to preach, and ordained.

I was also blessed to have a great pastor during my junior high and high school years named Carol Gilbert. "Gilly" was the pastor at the First United Methodist Church in Lamont, Oklahoma. He gave me my first Study Bible, and my first opportunities to participate in ministry. I am truly thankful for people like Gordon and Anita Heusel, Bob and Joyce Landis, and Rod and Diana Reese who taught me in Sunday School and volunteered to lead my youth group.

God used these people and countless others to influence my faith during my most formative years. However, concerning being discipled, I was not given the tools to cultivate my own spiritual growth nor was I taught how to use them until I was in college, where a Baptist campus minister named Brad Crosswhite became my friend. The first night we met we wrestled like a couple of barbarians on the floor of the Baptist Student Union, and then, for the next year and a half he taught me to wrestle with God's Word, my faith, and personal spiritual development. He discipled me.

This is why *Ascend* is in print today. Think about it. I was raised in church, and saved at age nine, but I was not systematically or intentionally taught how to grow in my faith for almost a decade. I believe this is part of the reason I have found it difficult to disciple people one on one in my own ministry.

In 2016, while preaching a series of sermons on the Great Commission, I was convicted of the fact that I had not discipled anyone in a long time. It also became painfully clear to me that the church I had been pastoring for almost ten years did not have any kind of discipling strategy. With that conviction fresh on my mind, I began researching discipleship material. After reading and trying to implement a few resources, I simply could not find a curriculum that fit me or my church. For this reason, I decided to develop material that would be clear, concise, and easy for me to use. I pray it will be useful for you too.

Ascend Should Be

Relational
Discipleship, by definition, requires a teacher/student relationship. Discipleship is not simply learning more information *about* Jesus. Discipleship is about becoming more *like* Jesus **(Matthew 10:24-25)**. This happens by talking through theological difficulties with someone, observing and participating in the Christian life together, and holding one another spiritually and morally accountable. How important is the relationship aspect of discipleship? It has been thirty years since our first wrestling match, and Brad is still a dear friend, a brother in ministry, and a mentor.

Preparatory
Ascend is not designed to be your final destination in discipleship. It is the jumping-off place. *Ascend* covers the basics in Christian doctrine and practice while at the same time teaching others how to study the Bible on his or her own.

Repeatable
In 2 Timothy 2:2 Paul says, "What you have heard from me in the presence of many witnesses entrust to faithful men, who will be able to teach others also." Ideally, after you have been discipled using *Ascend,* you should go through the workbook with someone who can then disciple others.

My prayer is that *Ascend* will be a tool you can use to help others climb the mountain of personal discipleship. May God bless you as you seek His face.

A disciple is not above his teacher, nor
a servant above his master.
It is enough for the disciple to be like his teacher...
Matthew 10:24–25

First Things First

An **E³ Encounter** is the weekly discipleship time you will share with a partner. During these encounters you will discuss what you have studied the previous week and continue to build your relationship by talking about your answers to the accountability questions found at the end of each chapter.

E³ stands for *Engage, Encourage,* and *Equip*

Pray. Ask God to lead you to the right person.

Make sure your partner has a copy of *Ascend* before you meet for your first discipleship time. Connect with your partner to set a time and date for your first **E³ Encounter**.

Use *"The Journey Begins"* on page 16 to be ready for your first **E³ Encounter**.

E³ Encounter pages are at the end of each chapter. These pages contain the accountability questions to ask when you get together and the assignment for the next session.

Go at your own speed. You do not have to finish a chapter a week.

There are three *In the Word* study sheets at the end of each chapter. Use these for personal Bible study and discuss them at your **E³ Encounter** each week.

Encourage your partner to write down questions they have throughout the week. Discussing these questions and learning how to study the Bible to discover the answers for oneself is crucial to the discipling process.

The Journey Begins

If anyone would come after me, let him deny himself
and take up his cross daily and follow me.
Jesus - Luke 9:23

My discipleship journey will require me to...

- Consistently read and study God's Word.
- Maintain a healthy prayer life.
- Serve others willingly.
- Participate regularly in worship.
- Give cheerfully.
- Share the Gospel.
- Hold my partner morally and spiritually accountable.
- Be morally and spiritually accountable to my partner.

_____   _____
Name   **Date**

Our First Meeting

Let's meet on _____ at _____
               Date   Time

at _____
                           Location

- For each meeting, bring your Bible, *Ascend* workbook, and a pen.

- Before your first meeting read the excerpts from *Costly Grace* by Dietrich Bonhoeffer and *Discipleship* by Eugene Peterson (**page 18-19**).

    — Be sure to write down any questions or comments.

- Begin praying now, asking God to use this discipleship study guide to help you grow as a follower of Jesus Christ.

Costly Grace

Cheap grace is the preaching of forgiveness without requiring repentance, baptism without church discipline, Communion without confession, absolution without personal confession. Cheap grace is grace without discipleship, grace without the cross, grace without Jesus Christ, living and incarnate.

Costly grace is the treasure hidden in the field; for the sake of it a man will go and sell all that he has. It is the pearl of great price to buy which the merchant will sell all his goods. It is the kingly rule of Christ, for whose sake a man will pluck out the eye which causes him to stumble; it is the call of Jesus Christ at which the disciple leaves his nets and follows him.

Costly grace is the gospel which must be sought again and again, the gift which must be asked for, the door at which a man must knock.

Such grace is costly because it calls us to follow, and it is grace because it calls us to follow Jesus Christ. It is costly because it costs a man his life, and it is grace because it gives a man the only true life. It is costly because it condemns sin, and grace because it justifies the sinner.

Above all, it is costly because it cost God the life of his Son: "ye were bought at a price," and what has cost God much cannot be cheap for us. Above all, it is grace because God did not reckon his Son too dear a price to pay for our life, but delivered him up for us. Costly grace is the Incarnation of God.

Dietrich Bonhoeffer, *The Cost of Discipleship*

Discipleship

It is not difficult in such a world to get a person interested in the message of the gospel; it is terrifically difficult to sustain the interest. Millions of people in our culture make decisions for Christ, but there is a dreadful attrition rate. Many claim to have been born again, but the evidence for mature Christian discipleship is slim. In our culture anything, even news about God, can be sold if it is packaged freshly; but when it loses its novelty, it goes on the garbage heap. There is a great market for religious experience in our world; there is little enthusiasm for the patient acquisition of virtue, little inclination to sign up for the long apprenticeship in what earlier generations of Christians called holiness.

Eugene Peterson, *A Long Obedience in the Same Direction*

- Get to know each other. Share a little bit about your life and your spiritual journey.
- Discuss goals: What would you like to see come out of our discipleship time?

Accountability Questions

- Are you praying?
- Are you reading?
- Are you serving?
- Are you giving?
- Are you worshiping?
  - — Are you going through any personal struggles I can pray about with you?
  - — Are you struggling with any sin I can pray about with you? **(James 5:16)**
  - — Is there a burden I can help bear? **(Galatians 6:9)**
- Discuss **Costly Grace** and **Discipleship**. (Page 18-19)
- Share prayer requests and pray together.

For Next Time

☐ Complete **Chapter 1, Saved By Grace.**

☐ Read the Bible every day.

☐ Pray every day.

☐ Do three *In the Word* Bible study pages.

☐ Memorize: _____ (See Appendix 1, Page 167)

Chapter 1 – Saved By Grace

YOUR TESTIMONY

Tell your story: How were you saved? How does being a Christian affect your life today?

_____

_____

_____

_____

_____

_____

_____

_____

_____

_____

_____

_____

_____

_____

_____

_____

_____

HOW GREAT A SALVATION

Read the verses below. They will help you
answer the questions on page 24.

1.) We are *saved* by **GRACE** alone. **(Ephesians 2:8-9)**

2.) We are *saved* by the **BLOOD** of Jesus Christ. **(1 John 4:10, Romans 3:23-25)**

3.) We are *saved* from **SIN, DEATH**, and **HELL. (Romans 3:23, Romans 6:23, Revelation 19:15)**

4.) We **CAN'T** *save* **OURSELVES. (Romans 3:10-12, Ephesians 2:4-5)**

5.) We are *saved* to a **NEW LIFE** in Christ. **(Romans 6:3-4, 2 Corinthians 5:17, Galatians 2:20)**

6.) *Salvation* is **SECURE** in Christ. **(1 Peter 1:3-5, Ephesians 1:13-14, John 10:27-30)**

BAPTISM AND THE LORD'S SUPPER

Baptism and sharing in the Lord's Supper remind and instruct us concerning the atoning death of Jesus Christ. Baptism and the Lord's Supper are also ways Christians publicly identify as followers of Jesus Christ and members of His body the church. A person should observe these ordinances because he or she has been saved, not in order to be saved.

Baptism

1.) Baptism is an act of obedience. **(Matthew 28:19-20)**

2.) It is how a new believer publicly confesses Jesus Christ as the Lord of his or her life. Through baptism, an individual is identified as a follower of Christ and a member of His church. **(Matthew 10:32-33, Romans 10:9)**

3.) It symbolizes the washing away of sins and the cleansing that comes through the blood of Jesus Christ. **(Acts 22:16, Isaiah 1:18, 1 John 1:7)**

4.) It symbolizes a believer's death and burial into Christ and resurrection into a new life in Jesus. **(Romans 6:3-4)**

The Lord's Supper

Read - **1 Corinthians 11:23-32**

When we share in the Lord's Supper:

- *Look Back*   We **REMEMBER** Jesus' atoning death on the cross.
- *Look Ahead*   We **PROCLAIM** the Lord's death until He returns.
- *Look Inward*   We **EXAMINE** ourselves to be certain we are walking in a right relationship with the Lord and others.

SAVED BY GRACE - QUIZ

Write **Ephesians 2:8-9** in your own words. _____
_____
_____
_____

True or False

T or F   I have to be a good person to be saved.

T or F   Salvation begins with the blood of Jesus and is completed by baptism.

T or F   Salvation changes me spiritually, but my every-day life stays the same.

T or F   Baptism and the Lord's Supper do not save a person.

T or F   We cannot lose our salvation; it is secure in Christ.

T or F   When we share in the Lord's Supper, it is a good time to examine our own heart.

T or F   Only the blood of Jesus Christ can atone for sin.

T or F   Baptism is an act of obedience that pubicaly identifies a new believer as a follower of Christ.

T or F   Because God is loving, eventually everyone will get to go to heaven.

Fill in the Blanks

For _____ have sinned and _____ of the glory of God. (Romans 3:23)

For the _____ of sin is _____, but the free gift of God is in Christ Jesus our Lord. (Romans 6:23)

And if anyone's _____ was not found _____ in the book of _____, he was thrown into the lake of _____. (Revelation 20:15)

But God _____ His love for us in that while we were still _____, Christ died for us. (Romans 5:8)

In Him you also, when you heard the word of truth, the _____ of your salvation, and believed in Him, were _____ with the promised Holy Spirit. (Ephesians 1:13)

In the Word

Date:

Text:

Lord, show me in Your Word what You want me to learn today.
Guide me, Holy Spirit, into all Truth. (John 16:13-14)

What is the main point of this passage?

Are there any specific commands to obey?

How does it apply to my life?

Are there any actions I need to take?

Notes:

_____

_____

_____

_____

_____

_____

_____

In the Word

Date:

Text:

Lord, show me in Your Word what You want me to learn today. Guide me, Holy Spirit, into all Truth. (John 16:13-14)

What is the main point of this passage?

Are there any specific commands to obey?

How does it apply to my life?

Are there any actions I need to take?

Notes:

_____

_____

_____

_____

_____

_____

_____

In the Word

Date:

Text:

Lord, show me in Your Word what You want me to learn today.
Guide me, Holy Spirit, into all Truth. (John 16:13-14)

What is the main point of this passage?

Are there any specific commands to obey?

How does it apply to my life?

Are there any actions I need to take?

Notes:

_____

_____

_____

_____

_____

_____

_____

_____

Accountability Questions

- Are you praying?

- Are you reading?

- Are you serving?

- Are you giving?

- Are you worshiping?

  — Are you going through any personal struggles I can pray about with you?

  — Are you struggling with any sin I can pray about with you? **(James 5:16)**

  — Is there a burden I can help you bear? **(Galatians 6:9)**

- Discuss your answers from Chapter 1.

- Review your ***In The Word*** study sheets.

- Quote memory verse.

- Share prayer requests and pray together.

For Next Time

❑ Complete **Chapter 2, Am I A Disciple?**

❑ Read the Bible every day.

❑ Pray every day.

❑ Do three *In the Word* Bible study pages.

❑ Memorize: _____ (See Appendix 1, Page 167)

Chapter 2 – Am I A Disciple?

DISCIPLES ARE <u>LEARNERS</u>

Matthew 10:24-25
A disciple is not above his teacher, nor a servant above his master. It is enough for the disciple to be like his teacher...

Mark 4:33-34
And with many such parables He spoke the word to them, as they were able to hear it; and He did not speak to them without a parable; but privately to His own disciples He explained everything privately.

Luke 11:1
Now Jesus was praying in a certain place, and when he finished, one of his disciples said to him, 'Lord, teach us to pray, as John taught his disciples.'

What is the goal of a disciple? _____
_____
_____

How do you plan to achieve that goal? _____
_____
_____

Using the verses above, list 3 characteristics of discipleship and define each in your own words.

_____
_____
_____
_____
_____
_____

DISCIPLES ARE <u>FOLLOWERS</u>

What do each of these verses imply about following Jesus?

Matthew 8:23-24
And when He got into the boat, his disciples followed him. And behold, there arose a great storm on the sea, so that the boat was swamped by the waves; but he was asleep.

Luke 18:28
And Peter said, "See, we have left our homes and followed you."

Mark 8:34
And calling the crowd to him with his disciples, he said to them, "If anyone would come after me, let him deny himself and take up his cross and follow me."

Mark 1:17
And Jesus said to them, "Follow me, and I will make you become fishers of men."

DISCIPLES ARE <u>SENT</u>

Matthew 10:1-5

[1] And He called to Him His twelve disciples… [5] These twelve Jesus *sent* out, instructing them…

Read the verses below and relate in your own words what they teach about being sent.

Matthew 28:19-20 _____

_____

_____

Acts 1:8 _____

_____

_____

COUNTING THE COST

Read **Luke 14:25-35**

Who is the audience in this passage? (v.25 and 35) _____
_____
_____

What is the central theme running through this passage? _____
_____
_____

- **<u>Love Jesus more than you love your FAMILY</u>. (v.26)**

	<u>Circle One</u>	
Who is the greatest focus of your love?	Parents	Siblings
	Spouse	Children
If I love Jesus more, I'll love my family less.	True or	False

- **<u>Love Jesus more than you love your LIFE</u>. (v.27)**

What does "bear your own cross" mean in our culture?

What did it mean to Jesus' original audience?

- **<u>Love Jesus more than you love your POSSESSIONS</u>. (v.33)**

Which worldview best describes you right now?

Circle one below.

Secular Worldview   My possessions are mine. They define me. They are the measure of life's worth.

Christian Pop-Culture Worldview   I own my possessions, but I will loan them to God when convenient.

Biblical Worldview   All of my possessions are a gift from God and belong to Him. I am only a steward of them.

What adjustments do you need to make to bring your view of material possessions in line with God's Word? _____
_____

In the Word	Date:
	Text:

Lord, show me in Your Word what You want me to learn today. Guide me, Holy Spirit, into all Truth. (John 16:13-14)

What is the main point of this passage?

Are there any specific commands to obey?

How does it apply to my life?

Are there any actions I need to take?

Notes:

_____

_____

_____

_____

_____

_____

_____

_____

In the Word	Date:
	Text:

Lord, show me in Your Word what You want me to learn today.
Guide me, Holy Spirit, into all Truth. (John 16:13-14)

What is the main point of this passage?

Are there any specific commands to obey?

How does it apply to my life?

Are there any actions I need to take?

Notes:

_____

_____

_____

_____

_____

_____

_____

In the Word	Date:
	Text:

Lord, show me in Your Word what You want me to learn today. Guide me, Holy Spirit, into all Truth. (John 16:13-14)

What is the main point of this passage?

Are there any specific commands to obey?

How does it apply to my life?

Are there any actions I need to take?

Notes:

_____

_____

_____

_____

_____

_____

_____

Accountability Questions

- Are you praying?

- Are you reading?

- Are you serving?

- Are you giving?

- Are you worshiping?

  — Are you going through any personal struggles I can pray about with you?

  — Are you struggling with any sin I can pray about with you? **(James 5:16)**

  — Is there a burden I can help you bear? **(Galatians 6:9)**

- Discuss your answers from Chapter 2.

- Review your *In The Word* study sheets.

- Quote memory verse.

- Share prayer requests and pray together.

For Next Time

- ❑ Complete **Chapter 3, Trained for Godliness.**

- ❑ Read the Bible every day.

- ❑ Pray every day.

- ❑ Do three *In the Word* Bible study pages.

- ❑ Memorize: _____ (See Appendix 1, Page 167)

Chapter 3 – Trained For Godliness

THE SPIRITUAL DISCIPLINES

Picture your life as a journey complete with mountain-top experiences, valleys of difficulty, and stretches of fairly smooth traveling. Think of the Spiritual Disciplines as spiritual exercises that keep you in shape for the journey ahead.

1 Timothy 4:7–8
[7] Have nothing to do with irreverent, silly myths. Rather train yourself for godliness; [8] for while bodily training is of some value, godliness is of value in every way, as it holds promise for the present life and also for the life to come.

What do you need to do to get spiritually healthy? How can you SPIRITUALLY stay "in shape"? _____
_____
_____

In what ways can the Spiritual Disciplines benefit your life?
(1 Timothy 4:8)
_____
_____

2 Timothy 3:5 and 2 Peter 1:5-9
What is GODLINESS ? *(Use the verses above to formulate your own definition.)*
_____
_____

Hebrews 5:14
But solid food is for the mature, for those who have their powers of discernment trained by constant practice to distinguish good from evil.

According to this verse, how can you tell if someone is mature in the faith? _____

_____

What kind of effort do you put into your relationship with the Lord?

_____

Bible Study

2 Timothy 3:16-17

Hebrews 4:12

Psalm 119:11

Prayer

Matthew 6:5-14

1 Thessalonians 5:16-18

James 5:13-16

Worship

Psalm 100:1-5

John 4:23-24

Hebrews 10:24-25

Simplicity

Philippians 4:11

1 Timothy 6:6-8

Proverbs 15:16

Stewardship

2 Corinthians 9:6-8

Malachi 3:8-10

Proverbs 3:9-10

SPIRITUAL DISCIPLINES

Solitude

Matthew 14:23

Luke 4:42

Mark 1:35

Fasting

Matthew 6:6-18

Acts 14:23

Philippians 3:19

Serving

1 Peter 4:10

Mark 10:42-45

Galatians 6:2

Evangelism

2 Timothy 4:5

Mark 1:17

Acts 1:8

Journaling

Deuteronomy 6:6-9

Isaiah 30:8

Job 19:23-27

Use the scriptures provided with each Spiritual Discipline to formulate one action step you can take to strengthen these areas in your life.

Bible Study _____   **Serving** _____

_____   _____

_____   _____

Prayer _____   **Evangelism** _____

_____   _____

_____   _____

Simplicity _____   **Journaling** _____

_____   _____

_____   _____

Worship _____   **Fasting** _____

_____   _____

_____   _____

Stewardship _____   **Solitude** _____

_____   _____

_____   _____

FIND THE SPIRITUAL DISCIPLINES

```
S U E F R Q R G C E R W N D D
F T T D D I N I V L Y P U M W
S Y E A U I S A F O Y Q J O A
Q A U W T T N U B A M B K O L
R L C S A G I P X D P H N S Y
L G A L E R Y L R N D V Y I L
W F N L P G D D O A Q B K M A
B Q I H Y A F S R S Y O I P G
E S X T W O R S H I P E D L N
M R P E P L H M T I Z W R I I
G N I L A N R U O J P I S C V
U N M G M X G M J Q C D F I R
Z N S H V F D M V N Q C Y T E
W T B I B L E I N T A K E Y S
G A Z R H X Q V S O L Q V K D
```

BIBLE INTAKE

SIMPLICITY

SOLITUDE

SERVING

EVANGELISM

JOURNALING

FASTING

STEWARDSHIP

WORSHIP

PRAYER

A WORD OF ENCOURAGEMENT

Practicing the Spiritual Disciplines is hard. You will struggle. The key is perseverance.

Like exercise, the Spiritual Disciplines will get easier the more you practice them.

You will experience benefits in this life and in the life to come. **(1 Timothy 4:7-8)**

The Spiritual Disciplines themselves are not the goal. A growing relationship with Jesus is. In fact, practicing the Spiritual Disciplines without love is hypocrisy. **(Matthew 23:23-28)**

Psalm 63:1
O God, you are my God; earnestly I seek you; my soul thirsts for you; my flesh faints for you, as in a dry and weary land where there is no water.

In the Word	Date:
	Text:

Lord, show me in Your Word what You want me to learn today. Guide me, Holy Spirit, into all Truth. (John 16:13-14)

What is the main point of this passage?

Are there any specific commands to obey?

How does it apply to my life?

Are there any actions I need to take?

Notes:

_____

_____

_____

_____

_____

_____

_____

In the Word	Date:
	Text:

Lord, show me in Your Word what You want me to learn today. Guide me, Holy Spirit, into all Truth. (John 16:13-14)

What is the main point of this passage?

Are there any specific commands to obey?

How does it apply to my life?

Are there any actions I need to take?

Notes:

_____

_____

_____

_____

_____

_____

_____

In the Word	Date:
	Text:

Lord, show me in Your Word what You want me to learn today. Guide me, Holy Spirit, into all Truth. (John 16:13-14)

What is the main point of this passage?

Are there any specific commands to obey?

How does it apply to my life?

Are there any actions I need to take?

Notes:

_____

_____

_____

_____

_____

_____

_____

Accountability Questions

- Are you praying?

- Are you reading?

- Are you serving?

- Are you giving?

- Are you worshiping?

  — Are you going through any personal struggles I can pray about with you?

  — Are you struggling with any sin I can pray about with you? **(James 5:16)**

  — Is there a burden I can help bear? **(Galatians 6:9)**

- Discuss your answers from Chapter 3.

- Review your *In The Word* study sheets.

- Quote memory verse.

- Share prayer requests and pray together.

For Next Time

❑ Complete **Chapter 4, By the Book – Part 1**

❑ Read the Bible every day.

❑ Pray every day.

❑ Do three *In the Word* Bible study pages.

❑ Memorize: _____ (See Appendix 1, Page 167)

BECOMING A STUDENT OF THE WORD

Often when people say they are "studying" the Bible, they should actually say "reading" the Bible. Studying takes time, concentration, and effort. In order to study you will have to make time, limit distractions, and acquire a few tools for the job.

When will be the best time for you to study your Bible? _____
_____

How much time will you need? _____

What will be your most common distractions? _____
_____

How can you eliminate those distractions for a short period of time?
_____

What can you do to improve concentration? _____
_____

What resources do you already use to study the Bible? _____
_____

The difference between studying the Bible and reading the Bible can be compared to the difference between being a detective and a patrol officer. The patrol officer covers many miles and sees a multitude of events. A detective moves slowly, focuses on one crime scene, imagines the crime taking place (context), and examines every clue.

Which are you? A **DETECTIVE** or a **PATROL OFFICER**? Explain why.
_____
_____
_____

KEY TERMS AND DEFINITIONS

WARNING: Do not quickly scan the information on the next two pages. Take time to develop a working understanding of these terms and definitions; they are the foundations upon which good Bible study methods will be built.

INSPIRATION (2 Timothy 3:16-17 and 2 Peter 1:20-21)
The writers of the Bible were guided by the Holy Spirit to communicate exactly what God wanted us to know about Him. The Greek word **inspired** used in the New Testament literally means **"God-breathed."**

PRESERVATION (Matthew 5:18)
Although we do not have the original autographs (very first copies) of Scripture, God in His sovereignty has preserved the Scriptures for us exactly as He intended. In fact, there are thousands of surviving copies and fragments of the Bible from only hundreds of years after the New Testament was produced, which is more than any other book from antiquity. **(Geisler 532)**

ILLUMINATION (John 16:13 and Psalm 25:5)
The Holy Spirit guides Christians into all truth as they read the Bible. This means God will give readers wisdom and understanding as they study the Scriptures.

INERRANCY AND INFALLIBILITY (2 Timothy 3:16)

The Bible is complete and free from error. What skeptics call contradictions are copy errors that are the result of centuries of transmission and translation. An example of a copy error would be changing "Jesus Christ our Lord" to "Our Lord Jesus Christ." Furthermore, "copy errors' do not compromise the integrity of the Scriptures, and no major doctrinal issues are affected by the copyist errors. In fact, *The Baker Encyclopedia of Christian Apologetics* says that compared to other ancient manuscripts the Bible is 99.5% accurate. **(Geisler 533)**

Interpretation

Discerning the meaning of the author's original message to his original audience.

Application

Applying to your every day life the truth the author was conveying to his original audience.

THREE APPROACHES TO INTERPRETING SCRIPTURE

Allegorical Approach
The **READER DISCERNS** hidden or secondary meanings in the text.

> *Example*: In **John 2:1**, "third day" represent the resurrection. In **John 2:6**, the "six stone water pots" represent the six days of creation.

There are times when Scripture is interpreted allegorically, but those times are obvious, as in **Galatians 4:21-31 and Revelation 12:1-6**

Reader-Response Approach
The **READER DECIDES** the author's original intent. The basis for interpreting Scripture this way is not the text, but the reader's personal experience.

> *Example*: This is when you hear phrases in a group Bible study like: "What does that mean to you?" or "How does that make you feel?"

Historical Grammatical Approach
The **READER DISCOVERS** the author's original intent by understanding the context of the Scripture passage as well as the history, culture, geography, and grammar of the text.

> *Example*: In **Romans 10:9**, Paul instructs Christians to "confess that Jesus is Lord" in a city and time when refusing to confess "Caesar is Lord" was a capital offense.

MATCH THE TERM TO THE DEFINITION

Application   Discerning the meaning of the
                            author's original message.

Inspiration   God's ability to maintain the
                            Scriptures throughout the centuries.

Historical   Understanding how the Bible applies
Grammatical   to your life today.

Illumination   Free from errors.

Interpretation   You decide what the Bible verse
                            means.

Reader-Response   Secondary or hidden meanings in a
                            Bible verse.

Preservation   The Bible is God-breathed.

Inerrancy   Interpreting the Bible grammatically
                            and in the context of the culture,
                            geography, and history of when it was
                            written.

Allegorical   Enlightened by God to understand the
                            Scriptures.

In the Word	Date:
	Text:

Lord, show me in Your Word what You want me to learn today. Guide me, Holy Spirit, into all Truth. (John 16:13-14)

What is the main point of this passage?

Are there any specific commands to obey?

How does it apply to my life?

Are there any actions I need to take?

Notes:

_____

_____

_____

_____

_____

_____

_____

In the Word	Date:
	Text:

Lord, show me in Your Word what You want me to learn today. Guide me, Holy Spirit, into all Truth. (John 16:13-14)

What is the main point of this passage?

Are there any specific commands to obey?

How does it apply to my life?

Are there any actions I need to take?

Notes:

_____

_____

_____

_____

_____

_____

_____

In the Word

Date:

Text:

Lord, show me in Your Word what You want me to learn today. Guide me, Holy Spirit, into all Truth. (John 16:13-14)

What is the main point of this passage?

Are there any specific commands to obey?

How does it apply to my life?

Are there any actions I need to take?

Notes:

_____

_____

_____

_____

_____

_____

_____

Accountability Questions

- Are you praying?

- Are you reading?

- Are you serving?

- Are you giving?

- Are you worshiping?

  — Are you going through any personal struggles I can pray about with you?

  — Are you struggling with any sin I can pray about with you? **(James 5:16)**

  — Is there a burden I can help bear? **(Galatians 6:9)**

- Discuss your answers from chapter 4.

- Review your *In The Word* study sheets.

- Quote memory verse.

- Share prayer requests and pray together.

For Next Time

☐ Complete **Chapter 5, By the Book – Part 2**

☐ Read the Bible every day.

☐ Pray every day.

☐ Do three *In the Word* Bible study pages.

☐ Memorize: _____ (See Appendix 1, Page 167)

Chapter 5 – By the Book - Part 2

THE BENEFIT OF KNOWING THE AUTHOR

Several years ago a church member named Arline Bolerjack gave my wife a cookbook. It was not just any cookbook. It was her cookbook. Arline was the author. To this day, **Something Special** sits on the shelf with our other cookbooks and it is still our go-to cookbook. Arline is with the Lord now, but before she passed away, Dustie had the benefit of calling Arline any time she needed help or did not understand the recipe instructions. Imagine how helpful it was to know the author.

You and I have this same privilege when it comes to the Bible. We know the Author and He promises to lead and guide us into all truth. **(John 16:13, Psalm 25:5)**

> **The best way to know the meaning of any written communication is to ask the author.**

START WITH PRAYER

Psalm 119:18
Open my _____, that I may _____ wonderous things out of Your law.

James 1:5
If any of you lacks wisdom, let him _____ God, who gives generously to all without _____, and it will be given him.

UNDERSTANDING THE SCRIPTURES

Luke 24:45
Then he _____ their minds to understand the Scriptures.

Ephesians 1:16–18
[16] I do not cease to give thanks for you, remembering you in my prayers, [17] that the God of our Lord Jesus Christ, the Father of glory, may give you the Spirit of wisdom and of revelation in the knowledge of him, [18] having the eyes of your hearts enlightened, that you may know what is the hope to which he has called you, what are the riches of his glorious inheritance in the saints.

How can you have the spirit of wisdom? _____
_____

THE ART OF OBSERVATION

- Take your time. Read for depth, not distance.

- Read the same passage many times in different versions.

- Let the words mean what the words mean.

- Start with the obvious. Obvious does not mean shallow; it probably means right. As you read, mark things like:

    * People

    * Places

    * Events

    * Repeated words and phrases

    * Action Verbs

* Lists (Like the character of a deacon in **1 Timothy 3**)

* Important transition words (***Therefore*** and ***In order that***.)

IT'S AS SIMPLE AS – 5W'S

Ask questions like this when you study the Bible:

Who...   is the author?

is the audience?

What...   happened?

time is it? was said?

Where...   does this take place?

are they going?

have they been?

Why...   is this here?

did they do that? did they say that? did they go there?

When...   did this take place?

this was happening, what else was going on around the world? was this in correlation to the life and ministry of Jesus?

HOW MARTIN LUTHER STUDIED THE BIBLE

I study my Bible as I gather apples. First, I shake the whole tree that the ripest might fall. Then I shake each limb, and when I have shaken each limb, I shake each branch and every twig.

Then I look under every leaf. I shake the Bible as a whole, like shaking the whole tree. Then I shake every limb—study book after book. Then I shake every branch, giving attention to the chap- ters when they do not break the sense. Then I shake every twig, or a careful study of the paragraphs and sentences and words and their meanings. **Martin Luther (Tan 188)**

Mark the following passage by circling, underlining, or highlighting important information.

2 Corinthians 1:1–7

[1] Paul, an apostle of Christ Jesus by the will of God, and Timothy our brother, To the church of God that is at Corinth, with all the saints who are in the whole of Achaia: [2] Grace to you and peace from God our Father and the Lord Jesus Christ.

[3] Blessed be the God and Father of our Lord Jesus Christ, the Father of mercies and God of all comfort, [4] who comforts us in all our affliction, so that we may be able to comfort those who are in any affliction, with the comfort with which we ourselves are comforted by God. [5] For as we share abundantly in Christ's sufferings, so through Christ we share abundantly in comfort too. [6] If we are afflicted, it is for your comfort and salvation; and if we are comforted, it is for your comfort, which you experience when you patiently endure the same sufferings that we suffer. [7] Our hope for you is unshaken, for we know that as you share in our sufferings, you will also share in our comfort.

What is the main theme of this passage? _____

_____

Consider what you have marked. What are some words, phrases, or concepts you would want to study more in depth to better understand this passage? _____

_____

A Great Illustration of the Art of Observation.
Agassiz and the Fish - By the Student (Appendix 3, Pages 172-175)

In the Word	Date:
	Text:

Lord, show me in Your Word what You want me to learn today. Guide me, Holy Spirit, into all Truth. (John 16:13-14)

What is the main point of this passage?

Are there any specific commands to obey?

How does it apply to my life?

Are there any actions I need to take?

Notes:

_____

_____

_____

_____

_____

_____

_____

In the Word	Date:
	Text:

Lord, show me in Your Word what You want me to learn today. Guide me, Holy Spirit, into all Truth. (John 16:13-14)

What is the main point of this passage?

Are there any specific commands to obey?

How does it apply to my life?

Are there any actions I need to take?

Notes:

_____

_____

_____

_____

_____

_____

_____

In the Word	Date:
	Text:

Lord, show me in Your Word what You want me to learn today. Guide me, Holy Spirit, into all Truth. (John 16:13-14)

What is the main point of this passage?

Are there any specific commands to obey?

How does it apply to my life?

Are there any actions I need to take?

Notes:

_____

_____

_____

_____

_____

_____

_____

Accountability Questions

- Are you praying?

- Are you reading?

- Are you serving?

- Are you giving?

- Are you worshiping?

    — Are you going through any personal struggles I can pray about with you?

    — Are you struggling with any sin I can pray about with you? **(James 5:16)**

    — Is there a burden I can help bear? **(Galatians 6:9)**

- Discuss your answers from Chapter 5.

- Review your *In The Word* study sheets.

- Quote memory verse.

- Share prayer requests and pray together.

For Next Time

☐ Complete **Chapter 6, By the Book – Part 3**

☐ Read the Bible every day.

☐ Pray every day.

☐ Do three *In the Word* Bible study pages.

☐ Memorize: _____ (See Appendix 1, Page 167)

Chapter 6 – By the Book - Part 3

Understanding and Applying the Bible

It is a shameful thing to carelessly ignore the context. To deliberately violate the context is more than shameful; it is sinful, for it is a deliberate substitution of one's own words for the Word of God. The student of Scripture, though he may not understand the original languages, nevertheless has at his command the single most important tool -- the context. Let him use it diligently! **(McQuilkin 163)**

THE QUEST FOR CONTEXT

- Context can refer to the historical, cultural, or geographical setting in which a passage occurs. Context also refers to the verses that precede and follow the text you are studying.

- Observing the context forces the reader to examine the writer's overall flow of thought. What is the author trying to say? What is his main point?

- Context helps avoid "Proof-Texting." Proof-texting is using a Bible verse to make a point that the verse in question does not actually consider.

Fill in the Blank With the Right Context

Isaiah 53:5 But he was pierced for our transgressions; He was crushed for our iniquities; upon Him was the chastisement that brought us peace, and with His wounds we are healed.

Out of context: "With his wounds..." means the Messiah suffered to provide physical healing.

The right context: _____

Matthew 18:20 For where two or three are gathered in My name, there am I among them.

Out of context: Jesus is present at group prayer meetings.

The right context: _____

Ephesians 3:20 Now to Him who is able to do far more abundantly than all that we ask or think, according to the power at work within us.

Out of context: God can do more than we think or ask, therefore, ask big.

The right context: _____

Hint: *Figure out who the "we" and the "us" are. Look all the way back to **Ephesians 2:11** and the following verses to understand the context.*

HOW TO LOOK FOR CONTEXT

Use *1 Peter 4:12* as an example to complete this exercise.

Write down words or phrases in each of the following to help determine the central theme of **1 Peter**. Then capture the central theme of **1 Peter** in one or two sentences.

VERSE - 1 Peter 4:12

_____

_____

SECTION - 1 Peter 4:12-19

_____

_____

CHAPTER - 1 Peter 4:1-19

_____

_____

BOOK - 1 Peter 1:1—5:14

_____

_____

Write a sentence that expresses the main theme of 1 Peter.

_____

_____

_____

_____

OTHER SOURCES OF CONTEXT

What are some historical, cultural, or grammatical clues that help you understand each of these passages? Remember to use your observation skills by asking the **5 W's.**

Romans 13:1-7 (*Politics and Location*)

Galatians 3:15-18 (*Grammar and Old Testament*)

Jonah 1:1-3 (*Location*)

James 1:1-4 (*Historical Event*)

Mark 1:16-20 (*Culture and Location*)

Matthew 27:51 (*Old Testament Judaism*)

Acts 10:9-17 (*Culture and Religion*)

Mark 12:26-27 (*Grammar*)

"The Bible is meant to be bread for daily living, not cake for special occasions."
Anonymous

In the Word

Date:

Text:

Lord, show me in Your Word what You want me to learn today. Guide me, Holy Spirit, into all Truth. (John 16:13-14)

What is the main point of this passage?

Are there any specific commands to obey?

How does it apply to my life?

Are there any actions I need to take?

Notes:

_____

_____

_____

_____

_____

_____

_____

In the Word	Date:
	Text:

Lord, show me in Your Word what You want me to learn today. Guide me, Holy Spirit, into all Truth. (John 16:13-14)

What is the main point of this passage?

Are there any specific commands to obey?

How does it apply to my life?

Are there any actions I need to take?

Notes:

_____

_____

_____

_____

_____

_____

_____

_____

In the Word	Date:
	Text:

Lord, show me in Your Word what You want me to learn today. Guide me, Holy Spirit, into all Truth. (John 16:13-14)

What is the main point of this passage?

Are there any specific commands to obey?

How does it apply to my life?

Are there any actions I need to take?

Notes:

_____

_____

_____

_____

_____

_____

_____

Accountability Questions

- Are you praying?

- Are you reading?

- Are you serving?

- Are you giving?

- Are you worshiping?

  — Are you going through any personal struggles I can pray about with you?

  — Are you struggling with any sin I can pray about with you? **(James 5:16)**

  — Is there a burden I can help bear? **(Galatians 6:9)**

- Discuss your answers from Chapter 6.

- Review your *In The Word* study sheets.

- Quote memory verse.

- Share prayer requests and pray together.

For Next Time

❑ Complete **Chapter 7, By the Book – Part 4**

❑ Read the Bible every day.

❑ Pray every day.

❑ Do three *In the Word* Bible study pages.

❑ Memorize: _____ (See Appendix 1, Page 167)

Chapter 7 – By the Book - Part 4

OTHER SOURCES OF CONTEXT

Here then, is the real problem of our negligence. We fail in our duty to study God's Word not so much because it is difficult to understand, not so much because it is dull and boring, but because it is work. Our problem is not a lack of intelligence or a lack of passion. Our problem is that we are lazy (Sproul 20).

Hebrews 5:12-13

[12] For though by this time you ought to be teachers, you need someone to teach you again the basic principles of the oracles of God. You need milk, not solid food, [13] for everyone who lives on milk is unskilled in the word of righteousness, since he is a child.

What does your diet of Scripture look like? Circle the one which best applies to you.

A.) Crackers & Water   D.) Meat and Potatoes

B.) Milk   E.) Dessert

C.) Salad Bar

THREE BASICS OF BIBLE INTAKE

Hear God's Word   -   Read God's Word   -   Study God's Word

HEAR GOD'S WORD

Luke 11:28
Blessed rather are those who _____ the word of God and _____ it.

Romans 10:17
So _____ comes from _____ , and hearing through the _____ of Christ.

1 Timothy 4:13
Until I come, _____ yourself to the public reading of _____.

What are some ways you can increase hearing God's Word in your life? _____
_____
_____

When you listen to a sermon, are you a **PASSIVE** listener or an **ACTIVE** listener? Explain. _____
_____
_____

How can you **PARTICIPATE** in a sermon that is being preached?
_____
_____

READ GOD'S WORD

What three reasons do the following verses give for reading the Bible?

Matthew 4:4 _____
_____
_____

2 Timothy 3:16-17 _____
_____
_____

Psalm 119:105 _____
_____

Which obstacles make it hard for you to read the Bible?

Mark the following with YES, NO, or MAYBE.

What can you do to overcome these obstacles?

_____ Hard to understand.

_____

_____ Not enough time.

_____

_____ Don't know where to begin.

_____

_____ Don't have a Bible.

_____

_____ Don't see the need.

_____

_____ Other

_____

_____ Other

_____

TIPS FOR STUDYING GOD'S WORD

- Set aside a time to read.
- Use a Bible reading plan (See Appendix 2, Pages 168-171)
- Meditate on **ONE** word, phrase, or passage each time you read.
- Use a Study Bible
- Use a journal to take notes about what you read.
- Use study tools such as Bible dictionaries, commentaries, atlases, and encyclopedias.

Ezra 7:10
Ezra _____ _____ _____ to study God's Word.

Acts 17:11
The people of Berea _____ the Scriptures _____.

MEMORIZING SCRIPTURE

In your opinion, what makes memorizing Scripture so difficult?

_____

_____

Meditating on Scripture:

- Turn off your phone.
- Eliminate ALL distractions.
- Set a timer. Start small and work your way up. At first, three minutes of uninterrupted silence will seem like thirty minutes.
- Rewrite the passage in your own words.
- Pray through the text.
- Don't rush.
- Memorize a Bible verse to meditate on.

Reasons for Memorizing Scripture:

Spiritual Power **(Ephesians 6:17, Psalm 119, Matt. 4:1-11)**

Strengthened Faith **(1 Corinthians 10:13)**

Witnessing **(Matthew 10:19-20, Romans 10:17)**

Counseling **(2 Timothy 3:16-17)**

God's Guidance **(Proverbs 3:5-6)**

Tips for Memorizing Scripture:

- Have a plan.
- Write out the verses.
- Draw a picture.
- Think of an application.
- Be accountable to someone.
- Review and meditate on it every day.
- Use flashcards.

> **Psalm 119:148**
> My eyes are awake before the watches of the night, that I may meditate on your promise.

In the Word	Date:
	Text:

Lord, show me in Your Word what You want me to learn today. Guide me, Holy Spirit, into all Truth. (John 16:13-14)

What is the main point of this passage?

Are there any specific commands to obey?

How does it apply to my life?

Are there any actions I need to take?

Notes:

_____

_____

_____

_____

_____

_____

_____

In the Word	Date:
	Text:

Lord, show me in Your Word what You want me to learn today. Guide me, Holy Spirit, into all Truth. (John 16:13-14)

What is the main point of this passage?

Are there any specific commands to obey?

How does it apply to my life?

Are there any actions I need to take?

Notes:

_____

_____

_____

_____

_____

_____

_____

In the Word	Date:
	Text:

Lord, show me in Your Word what You want me to learn today. Guide me, Holy Spirit, into all Truth. (John 16:13-14)

What is the main point of this passage?

Are there any specific commands to obey?

How does it apply to my life?

Are there any actions I need to take?

Notes:

_____

_____

_____

_____

_____

_____

_____

_____

Accountability Questions

- Are you praying?

- Are you reading?

- Are you serving?

- Are you giving?

- Are you worshiping?

  — Are you going through any personal struggles I can pray about with you?

  — Are you struggling with any sin I can pray about with you? **(James 5:16)**

  — Is there a burden I can help bear? **(Galatians 6:9)**

- Discuss your answers from Chapter 7.

- Review your *In The Word* study sheets.

- Quote memory verse.

- Share prayer requests and pray together.

For Next Time

❑ Complete **Chapter 8, Let Us Pray**

❑ Read the Bible every day.

❑ Pray every day.

❑ Do three *In the Word* Bible study pages.

❑ Memorize: _____ (See Appendix 1, Page 167)

Chapter 8 – Let Us Pray

Acts 2:42

And they devoted themselves to the apostles' teaching and the fellowship, to the breaking of bread and the prayers.

Developing **DEVOTION** to Prayer
- See Also — **Acts 1:14, Acts 6:4, Luke 18:1-18**

Which word picture best describes your prayer life right now? Circle one.

A.) **A Hurricane** (Powerful and Devoted)
B.) **A Soaking Rain** (Healthy and Consistent)
C.) **A Gully Washer** (It Comes and Goes)
D.) **A Light Drizzle** (You Get the Picture)
E.) **A Drought** (Repent)

What can you do to be more devoted to prayer? _____
_____

KEEPING ALERT in Prayer

1 Peter 4:7
The end of all things is at hand; therefore be self-controlled and sober-minded for the sake of your prayers.

See Also
Matthew 26:41   Luke 21:36

What are some ways you can stay alert in prayer?

_____

_____

Some PRAYER REQUEST specifically mentioned in the Bible.

Psalm 122:6	The peace of Jerusalem
Colossians 4:2-3	Open doors for ministry
Matthew 9:37-38	People to share the Gospel
Matthew 26:41	To not enter into temptation
Luke 6:27-28	For your enemies
James 5:13-15	For the sick and the suffering
James 5:16	For one another
1 Timothy 2:1	For all people
1 Timothy 2:2	For government an world leaders

DIFFERENT TYPES OF PRAYER

PRAISE AND THANKSGIVING

God's Love - Mercy - Forgiveness
Omnipotence - Omniscience
Blessings - Salvation

CONFESSION AND REPENTANCE

Attitudes and Thoughts
Sins of Speech
(Lying, Gossip, Hurtful Speech,
Profanity)
Relationship Sins
Bitterness Grudges
Improper Relationships
Lack of Fellowship with other
Christians Problems in Family
Relationships

Sins of Commission
(Doing what you should not do.)
Stealing
Dishonesty
Sexual Impurity

Sins of Omission
(Not doing what you should do.)
Not Witnessing
Not Giving
Neglecting Prayer & Bible
Study
Disengaged Worship

> **Use the different types of prayer: Praise and thanksgiving, confession and repentance, petitions, intercessions, and meditation to develop your own prayer list.**

PETITIONS
Praying for Personal Needs
Make a list of prayer requests to bring before God.

Pray through the Fruit of the Spirit, that each might be evident in your life. **(Galatians 5:22)**

Love - Joy - Peace - Patience
Kindness - Goodness -
Faithfulness - Gentleness
Self-Control

Ask God for opportunities to serve others.

Ask God for opportunities to share the Gospel.

INTERCESSIONS
Praying for Others
Make a list of people to pray for:
People who need to be saved
People who are sick
People who are going through hard times
Your pastor and church staff

MEDITATION
Philippians 4:8, Psalm 46:10, and Psalm 62:1-2

Allow God to speak to you through the Word and His Spirit.
Memorize Scripture.
Sit quietly.
Read and meditate on Scripture.
Reflect on circumstances and what God is teaching you through them.

PRAYING THROUGH SCRIPTURE

An Example of Praying a Bible Verse

Proverbs 3:5–6

[5] Trust in the LORD with all your heart, and do not lean on your own understanding.

[6] In all your ways acknowledge Him, and He will make straight your paths.

"Heavenly Father, help me trust You with all my heart. I need Your guidance and direction to know what to do. I know You are infinite in wisdom, power, and love, and I can trust You to make my path straight. Thank You, Lord. Amen".

> **Praying through the Scriptures keeps our focus on God's will instead of our own.**

EPHESIANS 6:13-18

13 THEREFORE TAKE UP THE WHOLE ARMOR OF GOD, THAT YOU MAY BE ABLE TO WITHSTAND IN THE EVIL DAY, AND HAVING DONE ALL, TO STAND FIRM. 14 STAND THEREFORE, HAVING FASTENED ON THE BELT OF TRUTH, AND HAVING PUT ON THE BREASTPLATE OF RIGHTEOUSNESS, 15 AND, AS SHOES FOR YOUR FEET, HAVING PUT ON THE READINESS GIVEN BY THE GOSPEL OF PEACE. 16 IN ALL CIRCUMSTANCES TAKE UP THE SHIELD OF FAITH, WITH WHICH YOU CAN EXTINGUISH ALL THE FLAMING DARTS OF THE EVIL ONE; 17 AND TAKE THE HELMET OF SALVATION, AND THE SWORD OF THE SPIRIT, WHICH IS THE WORD OF GOD, 18 PRAYING AT ALL TIMES IN THE SPIRIT, WITH ALL PRAYER AND SUPPLICATION.

THE FULL ARMOR OF GOD

Fill in the Blanks Using Ephesians 6:13-18

TRUE or FALSE

If I put on the full armor of God, I won't have any more problems.

True   or   False

The armor of God will enable me to stand against the schemes of the Devil.

True   or   False

Praying in the Spirit at all times means I have to speak in tongues.

True   or   False

The _____ of Truth.

The _____ of Righteousness.

The _____ of the Gospel.

The _____ of Faith.

The _____ of Salvation.

The _____ of the Spirit, the

_____ of God.

In your quiet time, "pray on" the full armor of God. As you pray through these verses, picture in your mind putting on each piece of armor God provides for you.

In the Word	Date:
	Text:

Lord, show me in Your Word what You want me to learn today.
Guide me, Holy Spirit, into all Truth. (John 16:13-14)

What is the main point of this passage?

Are there any specific commands to obey?

How does it apply to my life?

Are there any actions I need to take?

Notes:

_____

_____

_____

_____

_____

_____

_____

In the Word	Date:
	Text:

Lord, show me in Your Word what You want me to learn today. Guide me, Holy Spirit, into all Truth. (John 16:13-14)

What is the main point of this passage?

Are there any specific commands to obey?

How does it apply to my life?

Are there any actions I need to take?

Notes:

_____

_____

_____

_____

_____

_____

_____

In the Word	Date:
	Text:

Lord, show me in Your Word what You want me to learn today. Guide me, Holy Spirit, into all Truth. (John 16:13-14)

What is the main point of this passage?

Are there any specific commands to obey?

How does it apply to my life?

Are there any actions I need to take?

Notes:

_____

_____

_____

_____

_____

_____

_____

Chapter 8 E³   ENCOUNTER

Accountability Questions

- Are you praying?

- Are you reading?

- Are you serving?

- Are you giving?

- Are you worshiping?

  — Are you going through any personal struggles I can pray about with you?

  — Are you struggling with any sin I can pray about with you? **(James 5:16)**

  — Is there a burden I can help bear? **(Galatians 6:9)**

- Discuss your answers from Chapter 8.

- Review your *In The Word* study sheets.

- Quote memory verse.

- Share prayer requests and pray together.

For Next Time

❑ Complete **Chapter 9, Worthy of Worship**

❑ Read the Bible every day.

❑ Pray every day.

❑ Do three *In the Word* Bible study pages.

❑ Memorize: _____ (See Appendix 1, Page 167)

Chapter 9 – Worthy of Worship

To worship God is to ascribe the proper worth to God, to magnify His worthiness of praise, or better, to approach and address God as He is worthy. (Donald Whitney)

Revelation 4:9-11

[9] And whenever the living creatures give glory and honor and thanks to Him who is seated on the throne, to Him who lives forever and ever. [10] the twenty-four elders will fall down before Him who is seated on the throne, and worship Him who lives forever and ever, They cast their crowns before the throne, saying, [11] "Worthy are You, our Lord and God, to receive glory and honor and power; for You created all things, and because of Your will they existed and were created."

What is Worship?

In your own words, what is worship?

_____
_____

Why do we worship?

_____
_____

> If you don't enjoy praising and worshiping God,
> you are going to hate heaven.

In your opinion, what are the most important aspects of worship. In the space provided formulate your list from most important to least important:

Praying   Singing   Announcements
Welcome Time *(Shaking Hands / Greeting)*
Preaching   Invitation   Offering
Scripture Reading
The Lord's Supper

_____
_____
_____
_____
_____
_____
_____
_____
_____
_____
_____
_____

What can diminish focus on God during worship?

_____
_____

Worship is the _____ response of someone who focuses on the attributes of God. (His **power**, **wisdom**, **love**, and **majesty**).

A.) Forced   B.) Natural   C.) Mindless   D.) Manufactured

> **Church Attender: "I didn't like the worship today."**
> **Me: "It's ok, we weren't worshiping you."**

John 4:23-25

[23] But an hour is coming, and is now here, when the true worshipers will worship the Father in spirit and truth, for the Father is seeking such people to worship Him. [24] God is spirit, and those who worship Him must worship in spirit and truth.

What does it mean to worship in spirit and truth?

SPIRIT	**TRUTH**	Mind
_____	_____	**Heart**
_____	_____	**Intellect**
		Emotion

What can be the result of worshiping in spirit without truth?

_____

_____

What can be the result of worshiping in truth without spirit?

_____

_____

How can we worship in spirit? _____

_____

How can we worship in truth? _____

_____

THE NEED OF PUBLIC AND PRIVATE WORSHIP

PUBLIC WORSHIP

What do you like best about going to church? _____

What do you like least about going to church? _____

Hebrews 10:24-25
[24] ...and let us consider how to stir up one another to love and good works, [25] not neglecting to meet together, as is the habit of some, but encouraging one another; and all the more as you see the Day drawing near.

Why do you think only about 20% of church members attend worship services on a regular basis? In other words, why do so many self-proclaimed Christians forsake assembling together?

_____

_____

_____

_____

_____

_____

PRIVATE WORSHIP

Luke 5:16
But He would withdraw to desolate places and pray.

How can you privately worship God? _____
_____

> **Hebrews 12:28–29**
> [28] Therefore let us be grateful for receiving a kingdom that cannot be shaken, and thus let us offer to God acceptable worship, with reverence and awe, [29] for our God is a consuming fire.
>
> Is the worship you offer to God acceptable? Explain your answer:
> _____
> _____
> _____
>
> Read Leviticus 10:1-2
>
> What sin did Nadab and Abihu commit?
>
> What was the result?
>
> Should we consider this when we worship?

In the Word	Date:
	Text:

Lord, show me in Your Word what You want me to learn today.
Guide me, Holy Spirit, into all Truth. (John 16:13-14)

What is the main point of this passage?

Are there any specific commands to obey?

How does it apply to my life?

Are there any actions I need to take?

Notes:

_____

_____

_____

_____

_____

_____

_____

In the Word	Date:
	Text:

Lord, show me in Your Word what You want me to learn today. Guide me, Holy Spirit, into all Truth. (John 16:13-14)

What is the main point of this passage?

Are there any specific commands to obey?

How does it apply to my life?

Are there any actions I need to take?

Notes:

_____

_____

_____

_____

_____

_____

_____

	Date:
In the Word	
	Text:

Lord, show me in Your Word what You want me to learn today. Guide me, Holy Spirit, into all Truth. (John 16:13-14)

What is the main point of this passage?

Are there any specific commands to obey?

How does it apply to my life?

Are there any actions I need to take?

Notes:

_____

_____

_____

_____

_____

_____

_____

_____

Accountability Questions

- Are you praying?

- Are you reading?

- Are you serving?

- Are you giving?

- Are you worshiping?

    — Are you going through any personal struggles I can pray about with you?

    — Are you struggling with any sin I can pray about with you? **(James 5:16)**

    — Is there a burden I can help bear? **(Galatians 6:9)**

- Discuss your answers from Chapter 9.

- Review your *In The Word* study sheets.

- Quote memory verse.

- Share prayer requests and pray together.

For Next Time

- ☐ Complete **Chapter 10, At Your Service.**

- ☐ Read the Bible every day.

- ☐ Pray every day.

- ☐ Do three *In the Word* Bible study pages.

- ☐ Memorize: _____ (See Appendix 1, Page 167)

Chapter 10 – At Your Service

1.) Circle the Spiritual Gifts in the passages to the right.

2.) Draw a square around the phrases that explain how the Spiritual Gifts relate to our lives.

God has given you special gifts, talents, and abilities to use to serve others and glorify Him. List a few of those gifts below:

_____
_____
_____
_____
_____
_____

What do you like to do or what are you passionate about? What do you love to do in your free time?

_____
_____
_____
_____
_____
_____

Romans 12:3–8

[3] For by the grace given to me I say to everyone among you not to think of himself more highly than he ought to think, but to think with sober judgment, each according to the measure of faith that God has assigned. [4] For as in one body we have many members, and the members do not all have the same function, [5] so we, though many, are one body in Christ, and individually members one of another. [6] Having gifts that differ according to the grace given to us, let us use them: if prophecy, in proportion to our faith; [7] if service, in our serving; the one who teaches, in his teaching; [8] the one who exhorts, in his exhortation; the one who contributes, in generosity; the one who leads, with zeal; the one who does acts of mercy, with cheerfulness.

1 Corinthians 12:4–11

[4] Now there are varieties of gifts, but the same Spirit; [5] and there are varieties of service, but the same Lord; [6] and there are varieties of activities, but it is the same God who empowers them all in everyone. [7] To each is given the manifestation of the Spirit for the common good. [8] For to one is given through the Spirit the utterance of wisdom, and to another the utterance of knowledge according to the same Spirit, [9] to another faith by the same Spirit, to another gifts of healing by the one Spirit, [10] to another the working of miracles, to another prophecy, to another the ability to distinguish between spirits, to another various kinds of tongues, to another the interpretation of tongues. [11] All these are empowered by one and the same Spirit, who apportions to each one individually as he wills.

Galatians 5:13–14

13 For you were called to freedom, brothers. Only do not use your freedom as an opportunity for the flesh, but through love serve one another. 14 For the whole law is fulfilled in one word: "You shall love your neighbor as yourself."

What is the motivation for serving?

How can you use some of the gifts and passions God has given you to share His love with the people around you?

---

1 Peter 4:10
As each has received a gift, use it to serve one another, as good stewards of God's varied grace.

- Look up the word STEWARD. What does it mean to be a steward?

- Are you a good steward of the gifts God has given you?

Why or Why Not?

Don't let the busyness of your hands become the burden of your heart.

Luke 10:38–42

38 Now as they went on their way, Jesus entered a village. And a woman named Martha welcomed him into her house. 39 And she had a sister called Mary, who sat at the Lord's feet and listened to His teaching. 40 But Martha was distracted with much serving. And she went up to him and said, "Lord, do you not care that my sister has left me to serve alone? Tell her then to help me." 41 But the Lord answered her, "Martha, Martha, you are anxious and troubled about many things, 42 but one thing is necessary. Mary has chosen the good portion, which will not be taken away from her."

How did Martha's serving affect her spiritually?

She was _____ (v.40)

She was _____ (v.41)

She was _____ (v.41)

How can you prevent this from happening in your life?

In the Word	Date:
	Text:

Lord, show me in Your Word what You want me to learn today.
Guide me, Holy Spirit, into all Truth. (John 16:13-14)

What is the main point of this passage?

Are there any specific commands to obey?

How does it apply to my life?

Are there any actions I need to take?

Notes:

_____

_____

_____

_____

_____

_____

_____

_____

In the Word	Date:
	Text:

Lord, show me in Your Word what You want me to learn today. Guide me, Holy Spirit, into all Truth. (John 16:13-14)

What is the main point of this passage?

Are there any specific commands to obey?

How does it apply to my life?

Are there any actions I need to take?

Notes:

_____

_____

_____

_____

_____

_____

_____

In the Word

Date:

Text:

Lord, show me in Your Word what You want me to learn today. Guide me, Holy Spirit, into all Truth. (John 16:13-14)

What is the main point of this passage?

Are there any specific commands to obey?

How does it apply to my life?

Are there any actions I need to take?

Notes:

_____

_____

_____

_____

_____

_____

_____

Accountability Questions

- Are you praying?

- Are you reading?

- Are you serving?

- Are you giving?

- Are you worshiping?

  — Are you going through any personal struggles I can pray about with you?

  — Are you struggling with any sin I can pray about with you? **(James 5:16)**

  — Is there a burden I can help bear? **(Galatians 6:9)**

- Discuss your answers from Chapter 10.

- Review your *In The Word* study sheets.

- Quote memory verse.

- Share prayer requests and pray together.

For Next Time

❑ Complete **Chapter 11, The Gift of Giving.**

❑ Read the Bible every day.

❑ Pray every day.

❑ Do three *In the Word* Bible study pages.

❑ Memorize: _____ (See Appendix 1, Page 167)

Chapter 11 – The Gift of Giving

Why should Christians be generous givers?

A.) Because the church needs their money.

B.) Because God needs their money.

C.) To get a blessing in return.

D.) Because Christians should be good stewards of all God has entrusted to them.

Proverbs 11:24
One gives freely, yet grows all the richer; another withholds what he should give, and only suffers want.

Luke 6:38
Give, and it will be given to you. Good measure, pressed down, shaken together, running over, will be put into your lap. For with the measure you use it will be measured back to you.

◊   Do you believe the Bible is the Word of God?   Yes   No

◊   Do you believe the Bible is reliable and true?   Yes   No

◊   Can you trust God's Word concerning your   Yes   No
     finances?

FILL IN THE BLANKS
Using 2 Corinthians 9:6-15

If you _____ sparingly you will _____ sparingly, and if
you _____ bountifully you will _____ bountifully. **(v.6)**

God _____ a _____ giver. **(v.7)**

Give as you have _____ in your heart, not _____ or
under _____. **(v.7)**

God will _____ your seed for sowing. **(v.10)**

God is _____ when we give. **(v.13)**

Thank God for His inexpressible _____ **(v.15)**

THE DANGER OF ROBBING GOD

Malachi 3:8-10

[8] Will man rob God? Yet you are robbing me. But you say, 'How have we robbed you?' In your tithes and contributions. [9] You are cursed with a curse, for you are robbing me, the whole nation of you. [10] Bring the full tithe into the storehouse, that there may be food in my house. And thereby put me to the test, says the Lord of hosts, if I will not open the windows of heaven for you and pour down for you a blessing until there is no more need.

Why do people not give faithfully and cheerfully to the Lord?	What is the result of robbing God? (v.9)
How do they view their poor stewardship?	What is the result of faithfully giving to God? (v.10)
How does God view it? (v.8)	What does God mean when He says, "put me to the test?" (v.10)

Many Christians claim *tithing* is an Old Testament principle. This may in fact be a true statement, but read **Luke 18:18-23** and compare and contrast the New Testament principle of giving with the Old Testament principle of tithing.

Old Testament	New Testament

PERSONAL GENEROSITY

> **Acts 4:34–35**
> There was not a needy person among them, for as many as were owners of lands or houses sold them and brought the proceeds of what was sold and laid it at the apostles' feet, and it was distributed to each as any had need.

Describe a time when someone's generosity met a need in your life.

Describe a time when your generosity met a need in someone else's life.

In the Word	Date:
	Text:

Lord, show me in Your Word what You want me to learn today. Guide me, Holy Spirit, into all Truth. (John 16:13-14)

What is the main point of this passage?

Are there any specific commands to obey?

How does it apply to my life?

Are there any actions I need to take?

Notes:

_____

_____

_____

_____

_____

_____

_____

In the Word	Date:
	Text:

Lord, show me in Your Word what You want me to learn today. Guide me, Holy Spirit, into all Truth. (John 16:13-14)

What is the main point of this passage?

Are there any specific commands to obey?

How does it apply to my life?

Are there any actions I need to take?

Notes:

_____

_____

_____

_____

_____

_____

_____

In the Word

Date:

Text:

Lord, show me in Your Word what You want me to learn today.
Guide me, Holy Spirit, into all Truth. (John 16:13-14)

What is the main point of this passage?

Are there any specific commands to obey?

How does it apply to my life?

Are there any actions I need to take?

Notes:

_____

_____

_____

_____

_____

_____

_____

Accountability Questions

- Are you praying?

- Are you reading?

- Are you serving?

- Are you giving?

- Are you worshiping?

    — Are you going through any personal struggles I can pray about with you?

    — Are you struggling with any sin I can pray about with you? **(James 5:16)**

    — Is there a burden I can help bear? **(Galatians 6:9)**

- Discuss your answers from Chapter 11.

- Review your *In The Word* study sheets.

- Quote memory verse.

- Share prayer requests and pray together.

For Next Time

❏ Complete **Chapter 12, Can I Get A Witness?**

❏ Read the Bible every day.

❏ Pray every day.

❏ Do three *In the Word* Bible study pages.

❏ Memorize: _____ (See Appendix 1, Page 167)

Acts 1:8

But you will receive power when the Holy Spirit has come upon you, and you will be my witnesses in Jerusalem and in all Judea and Samaria, and to the end of the earth.

Look up the noun form of the word WITNESS in a Bible dictionary or lexicon and write the definition below.

_____

_____

_____

_____

_____

How are you empowered to share the Gospel?

What does a witness do?

Where is your Jerusalem?

Where is your Judea?

Where is your Samaria?

Where is the end of the earth?

Acts 8:1–4

[1] And there arose on that day a great persecution against the church in Jerusalem, and they were all scattered throughout the regions of Judea and Samaria, except the apostles. [2] Devout men buried Stephen and made great lamentation over him. [3] But Saul was ravaging the church, and entering house after house, he dragged off men and women and committed them to prison.

[4] Now those who were scattered went about preaching the word.

Who are the "they" who were scattered about? _____

Why were "they" scattered? _____

What did "they" do when they were scattered? _____

Who did not go about preaching the Word? _____

How does this apply to Christians today? _____

Evangelism To Do List	The Plan
Pray Ask God to lead you to the right people. Ask God to give you boldness. Ask God to give you the words to say.	Look up each verse and write the meaning in your own words in the space provided. Romans 3:23 _____
Listen Listen for opportunities to talk about God. For example, if people are hurting, tell them you will pray for them and use this opportunity to share the Gospel with them.	_____ Romans 6:23a _____ _____
Ask Ask questions like: If you died today, would you go to heaven? Why should God let you into heaven? What do you think it takes to get into heaven?	Romans 5:8 _____ _____ Romans 6:23b _____ _____
Share Share Scriptures with them that explain how they can have eternal life in Christ.	Acts 26:20 _____ _____ Romans 10:9 _____ _____

1 Corinthians 9:16–17

[16] For if I preach the gospel, that gives me no ground for boasting. For necessity is laid upon me. Woe to me if I do not preach the gospel! [17] For if I do this of my own will, I have a reward, but if not of my own will, I am still entrusted with a stewardship.

Now use these verses to formulate your own Gospel presentation.

Note: "preach the gospel" literally means "to evangelize"

Define:

Necessity (v.16)

Stewardship (v.17)

In the Word

Date:

Text:

Lord, show me in Your Word what You want me to learn today.
Guide me, Holy Spirit, into all Truth. (John 16:13-14)

What is the main point of this passage?

Are there any specific commands to obey?

How does it apply to my life?

Are there any actions I need to take?

Notes:

_____

_____

_____

_____

_____

_____

_____

In the Word	Date:
	Text:

Lord, show me in Your Word what You want me to learn today. Guide me, Holy Spirit, into all Truth. (John 16:13-14)

What is the main point of this passage?

Are there any specific commands to obey?

How does it apply to my life?

Are there any actions I need to take?

Notes:

_____

_____

_____

_____

_____

_____

_____

In the Word

Date:

Text:

Lord, show me in Your Word what You want me to learn today.
Guide me, Holy Spirit, into all Truth. (John 16:13-14)

What is the main point of this passage?

Are there any specific commands to obey?

How does it apply to my life?

Are there any actions I need to take?

Notes:

_____

_____

_____

_____

_____

_____

_____

_____

Accountability Questions

- Are you praying?

- Are you reading?

- Are you serving?

- Are you giving?

- Are you worshiping?

    — Are you going through any personal struggles I can pray about with you?

    — Are you struggling with any sin I can pray about with you? **(James 5:16)**

    — Is there a burden I can help bear? **(Galatians 6:9)**

- Discuss your answers from Chapter 12.

- Review your *In The Word* study sheets.

- Quote memory verse.

- Share prayer requests and pray together.

For Next Time

❑ Complete **Chapter 13, We Need Help.**

❑ Read the Bible every day.

❑ Pray every day.

❑ Do three *In the Word* Bible study pages.

❑ Memorize: _____ (See Appendix 1, Page 167)

Chapter 13 – We Need Help

THE HOLY SPIRIT

In **John 14:16, 14:26, 15:26,** and **16:7** the Holy Spirit is called the *paracletos* in Greek. This word is translated to **Helper** in the ESV. The NIV and NLT have it as **Advocate**, the KJV has **Comforter**, and the RSV translates it to **Counselor.**

How does the Holy Spirit:

Help you? _____

_____

Comfort you? _____

_____

Advocate for you? _____

_____

Counsel you? _____

_____

Where does the Holy Spirit dwell, and why is it important? **1 Corinthians 3:16-17** *('you' is plural)* _____

_____

1 Corinthians 6:18-19 _____

_____

According to **John 16:7-15** the Holy Spirit will convict the world of:

- _____
- _____
- _____

John 16:7–15

⁷ Nevertheless, I tell you the truth: it is to your advantage that I go away, for if I do not go away, the Helper will not come to you. But if I go, I will send him to you. ⁸ And when he comes, he will convict the world concerning sin and righteousness and judgment: ⁹ concerning sin, because they do not believe in me; ¹⁰ concerning righteousness, because I go to the Father, and you will see me no longer; ¹¹ concerning judgment, because the ruler of this world is judged.

¹² I still have many things to say to you, but you cannot bear them now. ¹³ When the Spirit of truth comes, he will guide you into all the truth, for he will not speak on his own authority, but whatever he hears he will speak, and he will declare to you the things that are to come. ¹⁴ He will glorify me, for he will take what is mine and declare it to you. ¹⁵ All that the Father has is mine; therefore I said that he will take what is mine and declare it to you.

1.) Circle the word **Helper** in the passages to the right.

2.) Draw a square around the words **The Spirit of Truth.**

Why was it advantageous that Jesus would go away and send the Holy Spirit? _____
_____
_____
_____
_____
_____

The Holy Spirit will only be with us for a short time.
True   or   False

The Holy Spirit will help us remember Jesus' teachings.
True   or   False

The Holy Spirit is the Spirit of Truth.
True   or   False

People who are not Christians get the Holy Spirit.
True   or   False

John 14:16–17
^{16} And I will ask the Father, and he will give you another Helper, to be with you forever, ^{17} even the Spirit of truth, whom the world cannot receive, because it neither sees him nor knows him. You know him, for he dwells with you and will be in you.

John 14:25–26
^{25} These things I have spoken to you while I am still with you. ^{26} But the Helper, the Holy Spirit, whom the Father will send in my name, he will teach you all things and bring to your remembrance all that I have said to you.

John 15:26
^{26} But when the Helper comes, whom I will send to you from the Father, the Spirit of truth, who proceeds from the Father, he will bear witness about me.

John 16:7–15
^{7} Nevertheless, I tell you the truth: it is to your advantage that I go away, for if I do not go away, the Helper will not come to you. But if I go, I will send him to you. ^{8} And when he comes, he will convict the world concerning sin and righteousness and judgment: ^{9} concerning sin, because they do not believe in me; ^{10} concerning righteousness, because I go to the Father, and you will see me no longer; ^{11} concerning judgment, because the ruler of this world is judged.
^{12} I still have many things to say to you, but you cannot bear them now. ^{13} When the Spirit of truth comes, he will guide you into all the truth, for he will not speak on his own authority, but whatever he hears he will speak, and he will declare to you the things that are to come. ^{14} He will glorify me, for he will take what is mine and declare it to you. ^{15} All that the Father has is mine; therefore I said that he will take what is mine and declare it to you.

CIRCLE YOUR ANSWER

All Christians have the same spiritual gifts.
(Romans 12:4-6)   Yes   No

Spiritual gifts are given for the common good.
(1 Corinthians 12:7)   Yes   No

We empower our own spiritual gifts.
(1 Corinthians 12:11)   Yes   No

The Holy Spirit distributes the spiritual gifts   Yes   No
according to His will not ours.
(1 Corinthians 12:11)

Love is more important than spiritual gifts.   Yes   No
(1 Corinthians 13:1-3 and 13)

Spiritual gifts come in many forms and functions.   Yes   No
(Exodus 35:30-35)

SOMETHING TO THINK ABOUT WHEN CONSIDERING SPIRITUAL GIFTS.

There are good people who come down on both sides of the more controversial Spiritual gift questions. Namely the gifts of speaking in tongues, healing, miracles, and prophecy. (I have always wondered why there is not as much passion about the gifts of helping, serving, administration, and giving).

We must always let LOVE guide and constrain our conversation when we discuss issues like this with others. Getting angry and resorting to personal attacks is never the answer.

Instead, I would suggest allowing the Scriptures to speak for themselves. Read the passages that deal with the spiritual gifts

in context and in several different translations of the Bible. Give the Holy Spirit time to guide you to the truth He has for you first **(John 16:13),** before turning to commentaries and other resources.

> **1 Corinthians 14:26**
> What then, brothers? When you come together, each one has a hymn, a lesson, a revelation, a tongue, or an interpretation. Let all things be done for building up.

WHAT'S YOUR GIFT?

Place an X in the box next to the spiritual gifts you think you may have.

The following Spiritual Gifts are listed in 1 Corinthians 12:7-10, 1 Corinthians 12:28, and Romans 12:6-8.

Use these definitions of the Spiritual Gifts to mark your answers.

☐ Wisdom

☐ Knowledge

☐ Faith

☐ Healing

☐ Miracles

☐ Prophecy

☐ Discernment

☐ Tongues

☐ Interpreting Tongues

☐ Apostles

☐ Teaching

☐ Helps

☐ Administration

☐ Serving

☐ Exhortation

☐ Giving

☐ Leadership

☐ Mercy

Wisdom - Discerning, understanding, and applying Biblical truth.

Knowledge - Deep insight into God's Word that surpasses human reason.

Faith - Unwavering belief in God that leads to action.

Healing - Physical healing in response to prayer.

Miracles - Divine intervention in response to prayer.

Prophecy - Boldly proclaiming the Word of God.

Discernment - Recognizing if an individual or teaching is from God.

Tongues & Interpreting Tongues - Ability to speak in, or understand a language you do not know.

Apostles - Sent with a special commission from God.

Teaching - Explaining and applying God's Word.

Helps - The desire and ability to help others.

Administration - Organizational and ministry skills.

Serving - Supporting and assisting others in ministry.

Exhortation - Encouraging others with words and deeds.

Giving - Cheerfully and generously providing financial support for ministry and spreading the Gospel.

Leadership - Inspiring and leading a group to accomplish specific ministry goals.

Mercy - Sympathizing and comforting others who are suffering.

In the Word	Date:
	Text:

Lord, show me in Your Word what You want me to learn today. Guide me, Holy Spirit, into all Truth. (John 16:13-14)

What is the main point of this passage?

Are there any specific commands to obey?

How does it apply to my life?

Are there any actions I need to take?

Notes:

_____

_____

_____

_____

_____

_____

_____

	Date:
In the Word	
	Text:

Lord, show me in Your Word what You want me to learn today.
Guide me, Holy Spirit, into all Truth. (John 16:13-14)

What is the main point of this passage?

Are there any specific commands to obey?

How does it apply to my life?

Are there any actions I need to take?

Notes:

_____

_____

_____

_____

_____

_____

_____

In the Word	Date:
	Text:

Lord, show me in Your Word what You want me to learn today.
Guide me, Holy Spirit, into all Truth. (John 16:13-14)

What is the main point of this passage?

Are there any specific commands to obey?

How does it apply to my life?

Are there any actions I need to take?

Notes:

_____

_____

_____

_____

_____

_____

_____

Accountability Questions

- Are you praying?

- Are you reading?

- Are you serving?

- Are you giving?

- Are you worshiping?

    — Are you going through any personal struggles I can pray about with you?

    — Are you struggling with any sin I can pray about with you? **(James 5:16)**

    — Is there a burden I can help bear? **(Galatians 6:9)**

- Discuss your answers from Chapter 13.

- Review your *In The Word* study sheets.

- Quote memory verse.

- Share prayer requests and pray together.

For Next Time

❑ Complete **Chapter 14, Lord, Come Quickly.**

❑ Read the Bible every day.

❑ Pray every day.

❑ Do three *In the Word* Bible study pages.

❑ Memorize: _____ (See Appendix 1, Page 167)

Chapter 14 – Lord, Come Quickly

THE RETURN OF CHRIST

Reading about the "last days" in the Bible _____ me.
- A.) Excites
- B.) Scares
- C.) Confuses
- D.) Other _____

Explain your answer: _____
_____
_____
_____

Mark 13:32–37

[32] But concerning that day or that hour, no one knows, not even the angels in heaven, nor the Son, but only the Father. [33] Be on guard, keep awake. For you do not know when the time will come. [34] It is like a man going on a journey, when he leaves home and puts his servants in charge, each with his work, and commands the doorkeeper to stay awake. [35] Therefore stay awake—for you do not know when the master of the house will come, in the evening, or at midnight, or when the rooster crows, or in the morning— [36] lest he come suddenly and find you asleep. [37] And what I say to you I say to all: Stay awake.

According to **Mark 13:32-37** what is the most important aspect of the return of Christ?
_____
_____

Matthew 24:36-44 Jesus will return like:
_____

Matthew 24:45-51 Jesus will return like:
_____

Which one do you relate to more?
Why?
_____
_____
_____

JUST THE FACTS

Read each passage and write a short statement that
captures how the return of Christ applies to you.

Jesus Will Come Again
Revelation 22:7, 12, and 20

_____

_____

Jesus Will Return Unexpectedly
Mark 13:32-37 and 1 Thessalonians 5:1-4

_____

_____

Christians Will Be Caught up to Be With Jesus
1 Thessalonians 4:13-18 and 1 Corinthians 15:51-52

_____

_____

The Unbeliever Will Be Judged and Condemned
Revelation 20:11-15 and Matthew 13:36-43

_____

_____

Believers Will Give an Account of Their Lives
Matthew 12:36 and 2 Corinthians 5:9-10

_____

_____

Satan Will Be Finally and Forever Defeated
Revelation 20:10

_____

_____

In the Word

Date:

Text:

Lord, show me in Your Word what You want me to learn today. Guide me, Holy Spirit, into all Truth. (John 16:13-14)

What is the main point of this passage?

Are there any specific commands to obey?

How does it apply to my life?

Are there any actions I need to take?

Notes:

_____

_____

_____

_____

_____

_____

_____

_____

In the Word	Date:
	Text:

Lord, show me in Your Word what You want me to learn today. Guide me, Holy Spirit, into all Truth. (John 16:13-14)

What is the main point of this passage?

Are there any specific commands to obey?

How does it apply to my life?

Are there any actions I need to take?

Notes:

_____

_____

_____

_____

_____

_____

_____

In the Word

Date:

Text:

Lord, show me in Your Word what You want me to learn today. Guide me, Holy Spirit, into all Truth. (John 16:13-14)

What is the main point of this passage?

Are there any specific commands to obey?

How does it apply to my life?

Are there any actions I need to take?

Notes:

_____

_____

_____

_____

_____

_____

_____

_____

Accountability Questions

- Are you praying?

- Are you reading?

- Are you serving?

- Are you giving?

- Are you worshiping?

    — Are you going through any personal struggles I can pray about with you?

    — Are you struggling with any sin I can pray about with you? **(James 5:16)**

    — Is there a burden I can help bear? **(Galatians 6:9)**

- Discuss your answers from Chapter 14.

- Review your *In The Word* study sheets.

- Quote memory verse.

- Share prayer requests and pray together.

For Next Time

- ❏ Complete **Chapter 15, If You Love Me.**

- ❏ Read the Bible every day.

- ❏ Pray every day.

- ❏ Do three *In the Word* Bible study pages.

- ❏ Memorize: _____ (See Appendix 1, Page 167)

Chapter 15 – If You Love Me

THE COMMANDS OF JESUS IN THE GOSPELS

— As you read each command, circle the verbs and verb phrases in each command.

— Place a check in the box by commands you already consistently obey.

Matthew 4:17	☐	Repent. Turn from your sin.
Matthew 5:12	☐	Rejoice when you are persecuted.
Matthew 5:16	☐	Do good things to others that will glorify God.
Matthew 5:23–26	☐	Seek reconciliation in broken relationships.
Matthew 5:27–30, Matthew 18:7–9	☐	Deal with sin in your life.
Matthew 5:37	☐	Say what you mean.
Matthew 5:39–42	☐	Turn the other cheek.
Matthew 5:44	☐	Love and pray for your enemies.
Matthew 6:1	☐	Do not act religious in order to be seen by others.
Matthew 6:6–9	☐	Pray
Matthew 6:19–21	☐	Invest in the next world, not this one.
Matthew 6:25, Luke 12:22	☐	Don't worry about daily needs.
Matthew 6:33, Luke 12:31	☐	Seek God's kingdom and righteousness first.
Matthew 7:1, Luke 6:37–38	☐	Don't judge.

Matthew 7:5	☐ Take the log out of your own eye before you try to take the speck out of someone else's eye.
Matthew 7:7, Luke 11:9	☐ Ask, seek, and knock.
Luke 6:30	☐ Give to anyone who asks.
Matthew 7:12	☐ Treat others the way you want to be treated.
Matthew 7:15	☐ Beware of false teachers.
Matthew 9:37–38	☐ Pray that God will send out people to share the Gospel.
Matthew 10:16–17	☐ Use common sense and do what is right.
Matthew 10:26–33	☐ Don't be afraid to proclaim the Gospel.
Matthew 11:28–30	☐ Embrace Jesus' teachings.
Matthew 16:5–6	☐ Beware of becoming a hypocrite.
Matthew 16:24–26, Luke 9:23–25	☐ Deny yourself, take up your cross, and follow Jesus.
Matthew 18:10	☐ Do not despise people who appear to be insignificant.
Matthew 18:15–17, Luke 17:3	☐ Confront a fellow Christian who refuses to turn from sin.
Luke 20:22–26, Matthew 22:17–22	☐ Give to the government what belongs to it and give to God what belongs to Him.
Matthew 24:4–8	☐ Do not get led astray and don't become alarmed in the last days.
Matthew 24:41–44, Matthew 25:13, Mark 13:3-33, Luke 21:34–36	☐ Be alert and ready for Christ's return.

Matthew 26:26–28, Luke 22:17–19	☐	Share in the Lord's Supper.
Matthew 26:41	☐	Be spiritually alert and pray that you won't fall into temptation.
Matthew 28:19–20	☐	Make disciples.
Mark 11:24	☐	Believe in God.
Mark 11:25	☐	Forgive others.
Mark 16:15	☐	Proclaim the Gospel.
Luke 6:22–23	☐	Rejoice when people treat you badly for being a Christian.
Luke 6:27–31	☐	Love, pray for, bless, and give to those who hate you and mistreat you.
Luke 6:36	☐	Be merciful like God is merciful.
Luke 10:20	☐	Rejoice because your name is written in the Book of Life.
Luke 12:4–7	☐	Fear God, not men.
Luke 12:15	☐	Guard yourself against every kind of greed.
Luke 12:33	☐	Sell possessions and give the proceeds to those in need.
Luke 12:35–36	☐	Be ready for the Lord's return.
Luke 17:3	☐	Pay attention to how you live your life.
Luke 21:7–8	☐	Don't be led astray by people who claim to be the Messiah.
Luke 22:26	☐	Serve others.
John 4:35	☐	Look at the world around you and see that it is time to share the Gospel.
John 12:26	☐	Follow Jesus.
John 14:1, John 14:27	☐	Don't stress out. Don't let your heart be upset. Trust God.

John 14:10–11	☐	Believe that God the Father and God the Son are the same.
John 15:4	☐	Live in and stay connected to Jesus.
John 15:9	☐	Live in and stay connected to Jesus' love.
John 15:12	☐	Love one another.

Go back over the list and highlight the commands you genuinely struggle with.

Use the space below to think of ways you can incorporate these into your daily walk with the Lord:

- _____
- _____
- _____
- _____
- _____
- _____
- _____
- _____
- _____
- _____

In the Word	Date:
	Text:

Lord, show me in Your Word what You want me to learn today. Guide me, Holy Spirit, into all Truth. (John 16:13-14)

What is the main point of this passage?

Are there any specific commands to obey?

How does it apply to my life?

Are there any actions I need to take?

Notes:

_____

_____

_____

_____

_____

_____

_____

_____

In the Word	Date:
	Text:

Lord, show me in Your Word what You want me to learn today. Guide me, Holy Spirit, into all Truth. (John 16:13-14)

What is the main point of this passage?

Are there any specific commands to obey?

How does it apply to my life?

Are there any actions I need to take?

Notes:

_____

_____

_____

_____

_____

_____

_____

	Date:
In the Word	Text:

Lord, show me in Your Word what You want me to learn today.
Guide me, Holy Spirit, into all Truth. (John 16:13-14)

What is the main point of this passage?

Are there any specific commands to obey?

How does it apply to my life?

Are there any actions I need to take?

Notes:

_____

_____

_____

_____

_____

_____

_____

_____

Accountability Questions

- Are you praying?

- Are you reading?

- Are you serving?

- Are you giving?

- Are you worshiping?

    — Are you going through any personal struggles I can pray about with you?

    — Are you struggling with any sin I can pray about with you? **(James 5:16)**

    — Is there a burden I can help bear? **(Galatians 6:9)**

- Discuss your answers from Chapter 15.

- Review your *In The Word* study sheets.

- Quote memory verse.

- Share prayer requests and pray together.

For Life

- ❏ Read and study the Bible every day.

- ❏ Pray every day.

- ❏ Memorize one Bible verse a week. (See Appendix 1, 167)

- ❏ Share the Gospel with at least one person every month.

- ❏ Give cheerfully and generously.

- ❏ Serve others.

- ❏ Go through this book with someone else.

- ❏ Get together two or three times a year with your E^3 partner to catch up.

- ❏ Go to church, sing to Jesus, be an active listener of the sermon, serve somewhere, and smile and greet everyone around you.

- ❏ Help someone else "ascend the hill of the Lord."

DISCIPLE SOMEONE!

	Date:
In the Word	
	Text:

Lord, show me in Your Word what You want me to learn today. Guide me, Holy Spirit, into all Truth. (John 16:13-14)

What is the main point of this passage?

Are there any specific commands to obey?

How does it apply to my life?

Are there any actions I need to take?

Notes:

_____

_____

_____

_____

_____

_____

_____

_____

In the Word	Date:
	Text:

"Lord show me in Your Word what You want me to learn today. Guide me Holy Spirit into all Truth." (John 16:13-14)

What is the main point of this passage?

Are there any specific commands to obey?

How does it apply to my life?

Are there any actions I need to take?

Notes:

_____

_____

_____

_____

_____

_____

_____

_____

In the Word

Date:

Text:

"Lord show me in Your Word what You want me to learn today. Guide me Holy Spirit into all Truth." (John 16:13-14)

What is the main point of this passage?

Are there any specific commands to obey?

How does it apply to my life?

Are there any actions I need to take?

Notes:

_____

_____

_____

_____

_____

_____

_____

_____

In the Word	Date:
	Text:

"Lord show me in Your Word what You want me to learn today. Guide me Holy Spirit into all Truth." (John 16:13-14)

What is the main point of this passage?

Are there any specific commands to obey?

How does it apply to my life?

Are there any actions I need to take?

Notes:

_____

_____

_____

_____

_____

_____

_____

_____

In the Word	Date:
	Text:

"Lord show me in Your Word what You want me to learn today. Guide me Holy Spirit into all Truth." (John 16:13-14)

What is the main point of this passage?

Are there any specific commands to obey?

How does it apply to my life?

Are there any actions I need to take?

Notes:

_____

_____

_____

_____

_____

_____

_____

In the Word	Date:
	Text:

"Lord show me in Your Word what You want me to learn today. Guide me Holy Spirit into all Truth." (John 16:13-14)

What is the main point of this passage?

Are there any specific commands to obey?

How does it apply to my life?

Are there any actions I need to take?

Notes:

_____

_____

_____

_____

_____

_____

_____

_____

In the Word	Date:
	Text:

"Lord show me in Your Word what You want me to learn today. Guide me Holy Spirit into all Truth." (John 16:13-14)

What is the main point of this passage?

Are there any specific commands to obey?

How does it apply to my life?

Are there any actions I need to take?

Notes:

_____

_____

_____

_____

_____

_____

_____

_____

In the Word	Date:
	Text:

"Lord show me in Your Word what You want me to learn today.
Guide me Holy Spirit into all Truth." (John 16:13-14)

What is the main point of this passage?

Are there any specific commands to obey?

How does it apply to my life?

Are there any actions I need to take?

Notes:

_____

_____

_____

_____

_____

_____

_____

_____

In the Word

Date:

Text:

"Lord show me in Your Word what You want me to learn today. Guide me Holy Spirit into all Truth." (John 16:13-14)

What is the main point of this passage?

Are there any specific commands to obey?

How does it apply to my life?

Are there any actions I need to take?

Notes:

_____

_____

_____

_____

_____

_____

_____

In the Word

Date:

Text:

"Lord show me in Your Word what You want me to learn today. Guide me Holy Spirit into all Truth." (John 16:13-14)

What is the main point of this passage?

Are there any specific commands to obey?

How does it apply to my life?

Are there any actions I need to take?

Notes:

_____

_____

_____

_____

_____

_____

_____

_____

Evangelism Encounter

Name: _____ Date: _____

Location: _____

General description of the conversation:

How did the individual respond?

What effect did his/her response have on you?

Evangelism Encounter

Name: _____ Date: _____

Location: _____

General description of the conversation:

How did the individual respond?

What effect did their response have on you?

Evangelism Encounter

Name: _____ Date: _____

Location: _____

General description of the conversation:

How did the individual respond?

What effect did their response have on you?

Evangelism Encounter

Name: _____ Date: _____

Location: _____

General description of the conversation:

How did the individual respond?

What effect did their response have on you?

Evangelism Encounter

Name: _____ Date: _____

Location: _____

General description of the conversation:

How did the individual respond?

What effect did their response have on you?

Evangelism Encounter

Name: _____ Date: _____

Location: _____

General description of the conversation:

How did the individual respond?

What effect did their response have on you?

Evangelism Encounter

Name: _____ Date: _____

Location: _____

General description of the conversation:

How did the individual respond?

What effect did their response have on you?

Evangelism Encounter

Name: _____ Date: _____

Location: _____

General description of the conversation:

How did the individual respond?

What effect did their response have on you?

Evangelism Encounter

Name: _____ Date: _____

Location: _____

General description of the conversation:

How did the individual respond?

What effect did their response have on you?

Evangelism Encounter

Name: _____ Date: _____

Location: _____

General description of the conversation:

How did the individual respond?

What effect did their response have on you?

Appendix

Appendix 1
Memory Verses

- [ ] James 1:22
- [ ] Psalm 119:11
- [ ] 1 Corinthians 10:13
- [ ] Romans 15:13
- [ ] Deuteronomy 31:6
- [ ] John 15:7-8
- [ ] Proverbs 3:5-7
- [ ] 2 Corinthians 5:17
- [ ] 1 Peter 1:14-16
- [ ] Romans 8:28
- [ ] Genesis 1:27
- [ ] Ephesians 2:8-9
- [ ] 2 Corinthians 9:6-7
- [ ] Isaiah 64:6
- [ ] Hebrews 4:12
- [ ] James 1:19-20
- [ ] Romans 3:23
- [ ] Romans 6:23
- [ ] Romans 5:8
- [ ] Romans 10:9
- [ ] Acts 3:19

- [ ] Psalm 42:5
- [ ] Ephesians 2:10
- [ ] Matthew 7:21
- [ ] 1 Timothy 6:6
- [ ] Philippians 4:11-13
- [ ] Luke 12:15
- [ ] 2 Timothy 4:5
- [ ] Colossians 2:6-7
- [ ] Exodus 20:1-17
- [ ] Luke 10:27
- [ ] Matthew 6:24
- [ ] Acts 2:38
- [ ] Matthew 28:19-20
- [ ] Acts 1:8
- [ ] Isaiah 40:31
- [ ] James 1:14-15
- [ ] Hebrews 11:1
- [ ] John 1:1
- [ ] James 1:13-14
- [ ] Galatians 5:22-23
- [ ] 2 Timothy 3:16-17

- [ ] Hebrews 12:1-2
- [ ] Revelation 3:20
- [ ] 2 Chronicles 7:14
- [ ] 1 Peter 5:6-7
- [ ] 1 John 1:9
- [ ] James 3:2
- [ ] Proverbs 13:24
- [ ] 1 John 4:7
- [ ] John 11:25
- [ ] Romans 12:1-2
- [ ] Hebrews 12:1-2
- [ ] John 14:6
- [ ] John 4:23-24
- [ ] Psalm 23
- [ ] Luke 2:10-12
- [ ] John 6:35
- [ ] James 3:2
- [ ] Deuteronomy 6:4-9
- [ ] Malachi 3:8-10
- [ ] Philippians 4:4-7
- [ ] Micah 6:8

Appendix 2
Bible Reading Chart

Genesis	1	2	3	4	5	6	7	8	9	10	11	12	13	14	15	16
	17	18	19	20	21	22	23	24	25	26	27	28	29	30	31	32
	33	34	35	36	37	38	39	40	41	42	43	44	45	46	47	48
	49	50														
Exodus	1	2	3	4	5	6	7	8	9	10	11	12	13	14	15	16
	17	18	19	20	21	22	23	24	25	26	27	28	29	30	31	32
	33	34	35	36	37	38	39	40								
Leviticus	1	2	3	4	5	6	7	8	9	10	11	12	13	14	15	16
	17	18	19	20	21	22	23	24	25	26	27					
Numbers	1	2	3	4	5	6	7	8	9	10	11	12	13	14	15	16
	17	18	19	20	21	22	23	24	25	26	27	28	29	30	31	32
	33	34	35	36												
Deuteronomy	1	2	3	4	5	6	7	8	9	10	11	12	13	14	15	16
	17	18	19	20	21	22	23	24	25	26	27	28	29	30	31	32
	33	34														
Joshua	1	2	3	4	5	6	7	8	9	10	11	12	13	14	15	16
	17	18	19	20	21	22	23	24								
Judges	1	2	3	4	5	6	7	8	9	10	11	12	13	14	15	16
	17	18	19	20	21											
Ruth	1	2	3	4												
1 Samuel	1	2	3	4	5	6	7	8	9	10	11	12	13	14	15	16
	17	18	19	20	21	22	23	24	25	26	27	28	29	30	31	
2 Samuel	1	2	3	4	5	6	7	8	9	10	11	12	13	14	15	16
	17	18	19	20	21	22	23	24								
1 Kings	1	2	3	4	5	6	7	8	9	10	11	12	13	14	15	16
	17	18	19	20	21	22										
2 Kings	1	2	3	4	5	6	7	8	9	10	11	12	13	14	15	16
	17	18	19	20	21	22	23	24	25							
1 Chronicles	1	2	3	4	5	6	7	8	9	10	11	12	13	14	15	16
	17	18	19	20	21	22	23	24	25	26	27	28	29			
2 Chronicles	1	2	3	4	5	6	7	8	9	10	11	12	13	14	15	16
	17	18	19	20	21	22	23	24	25	26	27	28	29	30	31	32
	33	34	35	36												

Ezra	1	2	3	4	5	6	7	8	9	10			
Nehemiah	1	2	3	4	5	6	7	8	9	10	11	12	13
Esther	1	2	3	4	5	6	7	8	9	10			

Job	1	2	3	4	5	6	7	8	9	10	11	12
	13	14	15	16	17	18	19	20	21	22	23	24
	25	26	27	28	29	30	31	32	33	34	35	36
	37	38	39	40	41	42						
Psalms	1	2	3	4	5	6	7	8	9	10	11	12
	13	14	15	16	17	18	19	20	21	22	23	24
	25	26	27	28	29	30	31	32	33	34	35	36
	37	38	38	39	40	41	42	43	44	45	46	47
	48	49	50	51	52	53	54	55	56	57	58	59
	60	61	62	63	64	65	66	67	68	69	70	71
	72	73	74	75	76	77	78	79	80	81	82	83
	84	85	86	87	88	89	90	91	92	93	94	95
	96	97	98	99	100	101	102	103	104	105	106	107
	108	109	110	111	112	113	114	115	116	117	118	119
	120	121	122	123	124	125	126	127	128	129	130	131
	132	133	134	135	136	137	138	139	140	141	143	144
	145	146	147	148	149	150						

Proverbs	1	2	3	4	5	6	7	8	9	10	11	12	13	14	15	16
	17	18	19	20	21	22	23	24	25	26	27	28	29	30	31	
Ecclesiastes	1	2	3	4	5	6	7	8	9	10	11	12				
Song of Solomon	1	2	3	4	5	6	7	8								

Isaiah	1	2	3	4	5	6	7	8	9	10	11	12	13	14	15	16
	17	18	19	20	21	22	23	24	25	26	27	28	29	30	31	32
	33	34	35	36	37	38	39	40	41	42	43	44	45	46	47	48
	49	50	51	52	53	54	55	56	57	58	59	60	61	62	63	64
	65	66														
Jeremiah	1	2	3	4	5	6	7	8	9	10	11	12	13	14	15	16
	17	18	19	20	21	22	23	24	25	26	27	28	29	30	31	32
	33	34	35	36	37	38	39	40	41	42	43	44	45	46	47	48
	49	50	51	52												
Lamentations	1	2	3	4	5											
Ezekiel	1	2	3	4	5	6	7	8	9	10	11	12	13	14	15	16
	17	18	19	20	21	22	23	24	25	26	27	28	29	30	31	32
	33	34	35	36	37	38	39	40	41	42	43	44	45	46	47	48
Daniel	1	2	3	4	5	6	7	8	9	10	11	12				
Hosea	1	2	3	4	5	6	7	8	9	10	11	12	13	14		
Joel	1	2	3													
Amos	1	2	3	4	5	6	7	8	9							
Obadiah	1															
Jonah	1	2	3	4												
Micah	1	2	3	4	5	6	7									
Nahum	1	2	3														
Habakkuk	1	2	3														
Zephaniah	1	2	3														
Haggai	1	2															
Zechariah	1	2	3	4	5	6	7	8	9	10	11	12	13	14		
Malachi	1	2	3	4												

Matthew	1	2	3	4	5	6	7	8	9	10	11	12	13	14	15	16
	17	18	19	20	21	22	23	24	25	26	27	28				
Mark	1	2	3	4	5	6	7	8	9	10	11	12	13	14	15	16
Luke	1	2	3	4	5	6	7	8	9	10	11	12	13	14	15	16
	17	18	19	20	21	22	23	24								
John	1	2	3	4	5	6	7	8	9	10	11	12	13	14	15	16
	17	18	19	20	21											

Acts	1	2	3	4	5	6	7	8	9	10	11	12	13	14	15	16
Romans	1	2	3	4	5	6	7	8	9	10	11	12	13	14	15	16
1 Corinthians	1	2	3	4	5	6	7	8	9	10	11	12	13	14	15	16
2 Corinthians	1	2	3	4	5	6	7	8	9	10	11	12	13			
Galatians	1	2	3	4	5	6										
Ephesians	1	2	3	4	5	6										
Philippians	1	2	3	4												
Colossians	1	2	3	4												
1 Thessalonians	1	2	3	4	5											
2 Thessalonians	1	2	3													
1 Timothy	1	2	3	4	5	6										
2 Timothy	1	2	3	4												
Titus	1	2	3														
Philemon	1															
Hebrews	1	2	3	4	5	6	7	8	9	10	11	12	13			
James	1	2	3	4	5											
1 Peter	1	2	3	4	5											
2 Peter	1	2	3													
1 John	1	2	3	4	5											
2 John	1															
3 John	1															
Jude	1															
Revelation	1	2	3	4	5	6	7	8	9	10	11	12	13	14	15	16
	17	18	19	20	21	22										

Appendix 3
Agassiz and the Fish
by a Student

It was more than fifteen years ago that I entered the laboratory of Professor Agassiz, and told him I had enrolled my name in the scientific school as a student of natural history. He asked me a few questions about my object in coming, my antecedents generally, the mode in which I afterwards proposed to use the knowledge I might acquire, and finally, whether I wished to study any special branch. To the latter I replied that while I wished to be well grounded in all departments of zoology, I purposed to devote myself specially to insects.

'When do you wish to begin?' he asked.

'Now,' I replied.

This seemed to please him, and with an energetic "Very well," he reached from a shelf a huge jar of specimens in yellow alcohol.

"Take this fish," he said, "and look at it; we call it a Haemulon; by and by I will ask what you have seen."

With that he left me. . . . I was conscious of a passing feeling of disappointment, for gazing at a fish did not commend itself to an ardent entomologist. . . . .

In ten minutes I had seen all that could be seen in that fish, and started in search of the professor, who had, however, left the museum; and when I returned, after lingering over some of the odd animals stored in the upper apartment, my specimen was dry all over. I dashed the fluid over the fish as if to resuscitate it from a fainting-fit, and looked with anxiety for a return of a normal, sloppy appearance. This little excitement over, nothing was to be done but return to a steadfast gaze at my mute companion. Half an hour passed, an hour, another hour; the fish began to look loathsome. I turned it over and around; looked it in the face—ghastly; from behind, beneath, above, sideways, at a three-quarters view—

just as ghastly. I was in despair; at an early hour, I concluded that lunch was necessary; so with infinite relief, the fish was carefully replaced in the jar, and for an hour I was free.

On my return, I learned that Professor Agassiz had been at the museum, but had gone and would not return for several hours. My fellow students were too busy to be disturbed by continued conversation. Slowly I drew forth that hideous fish, and with a feeling of desperation again looked at it. I might not use a magnifying glass; instruments of all kinds were interdicted. My two hands, my two eyes, and the fish; it seemed a most limited field. I pushed my fingers down its throat to see how sharp its teeth were. I began to count the scales in the different rows until I was convinced that that was nonsense. At last a happy thought struck me—I would draw the fish; and now with surprise I began to discover new features in the creature. Just then the professor returned.

"That is right," said he, "a pencil is one of the best eyes. I am glad to notice, too, that you keep your specimen wet and your bottle corked."

With these encouraging words he added— "Well, what is it like?"

He listened attentively to my brief rehearsal of the structure of parts whose names were still unknown to me; the fringed gill-arches and movable operculum; the pores of the head, fleshly lips, and lidless eyes; the lateral line, the spinous fin, and forked tail; the compressed and arched body. When I had finished, he waited as if expecting more, and then, with an air of disappointment:

"You have not looked very carefully; why," he continued, more earnestly, "you haven't seen one of the most conspicuous features of the animal, which is as plainly before your eyes as the fish itself. Look again; look again!" And he left me to my misery.

I was piqued; I was mortified. Still more of that wretched fish? But now I set myself to the task with a will, and discovered one new thing after another, until I saw how just the professor's criticism had been. The afternoon passed quickly, and when, towards its close, the professor inquired,

"Do you see it yet?"

"No," I replied. "I am certain I do not, but I see how little I saw before."

"That is next best," said he earnestly, "but I won't hear you now; put away your fish and go home; perhaps you will be ready with a better answer in the morning. I will examine you before you look at the fish."

This was disconcerting; not only must I think of my fish all night, studying, without the object before me, what this unknown but most visible feature might be, but also, without reviewing my new discoveries, I must give an exact account of them the next day. I had a bad memory; so I walked home by Charles River in a distracted state, with my two perplexities.

The cordial greeting from the professor the next morning was reassuring; here was a man who seemed to be quite as anxious as I that I should see for myself what he saw.

"Do you perhaps mean," I asked, "that the fish has symmetrical sides with paired organs?"

His thoroughly pleased, "Of course, of course!" repaid the wakeful hours of the previous night.

After he had discoursed most happily and enthusiastically—as he always did—upon the importance of this point, I ventured to ask what I should do next.

"Oh, look at your fish!" he said, and left me again to my own devices. In a little more than an hour he returned and heard my new catalogue.

"That is good, that is good!" he repeated, "but that is not all; go on." And so for three long days, he placed that fish before my eyes, forbidding me to look at anything else, or to use any artificial aid. "Look, look, look," was his repeated injunction.

This was the best entomological lesson I ever had—a lesson whose influence was extended to the details of every subsequent study; a legacy the professor has left to me, as he left it to many others, of inestimable value, which we could not buy, with which we cannot part. . . .

The fourth day a second fish of the same group was placed beside the first, and I was bidden to point out the resemblances and differences between the two; another and another followed, until the entire family lay before me, and a whole legion of jars covered the table and surrounding shelves; the odor had become a pleasant perfume; and even now, the sight of an old six-inch worm-eaten cork brings fragrant memories!

The whole group of Haemulons was thus brought into review; and whether engaged upon the dissection of the internal organs, preparation and examination of the bony framework, or the description of the various parts, Agassiz's training in the method of observing facts in their orderly arrangement, was ever accompanied by the urgent exhortation not to be content with them.

"Facts are stupid things," he would say, "until brought into connection with some general law."

At the end of eight months, it was almost with reluctance that I left these friends and turned to insects; but what I gained by this outside experience has been of greater value than years of later investigation in my favorite groups. *(Scudder, 450-454)*

Resources

Bonhoeffer, Dietrich, *The Cost of Discipleship*. (New York: Macmillian Co., 1965) 47-48.

Geisler, Norman L., *"New Testament Manuscripts,"* Baker Encyclopedia of Christian Apologetics, Baker Reference Library (Grand Rapids, MI: Baker Books, 1999), 533.

McQuilkin, Robertson, *Understanding and Applying the Bible.* (Chicago, IL: Moody Publishers, 1983) 163.

Peterson, Eugene, *A Long Obedience in the Same Direction*. (Downers Grove, IL: InterVarsity Press, 1980) 16.

Scudder, Samuel, *American Poems* (3rd Edition.: Boston: Houghton, Osgood & Co., 1879), 450-454.

Sproul, R.C., *Knowing Scripture*. (Downers Grove, IL: InterVarsity Press, 1977) 20.

Tan, Paul Lee, *Encyclopedia of 7700 Illustrations: Signs of the Times* (Garland, TX: Bible Communications, Inc., 1996), 188.

Whitney, Donald, *Spiritual Disciplines for the Christian Life* (Colorado Springs, CO: NavPress, 1991), 87.